No one else

can match the effectiveness, the simplicity, or the appeal of the

SPECTRUM READING SERIES

Students gain meaningful practice—independently

With the SPECTRUM READING SERIES students not only get the practice they need in essential reading skills, they also enjoy being able to do it on their own.

In grades one through six, each lesson features an illustrated story followed by exercises in comprehension and basic reading skills. Because the same format is used consistently throughout, your students will have little trouble doing the lessons independently. And each two-page lesson can be finished easily in one class period.

Students develop and refine key reading skills.

- **Comprehension** exercises help students go beyond understanding of facts and details to drawing conclusions, predicting outcomes, identifying cause and effect, and developing other higher level comprehension skills.
- **Vocabulary development** builds on words from the reading selections. In addition to learning synonyms, antonyms, and words with multiple meanings, students develop sight vocabulary and learn to use context as a clue for meaning.
- **Decoding** exercises refine students' abilities to "attack" and understand new reading words.
- **Study skills** are developed by helping students apply their reading skills to new tasks, such as using reference materials, reading graphs, and applying other everyday life skills.

Reading selections captivate and motivate.

Students get their best reading practice by actually reading. That's why the selections in the SPECTRUM READING SERIES, in addition to offering practice in skills, also motivate students to read—just for fun.

Students quickly become friends with the characters in these entertaining stories. And they enjoy new levels of reading success—thanks in part to carefully controlled vocabulary and readability as well as beautiful illustrations.

The program adapts completely to any teaching situation.

The SPECTRUM READING SERIES can be used in many different ways.

- For the whole class . . . for intensive reinforcement of reading skills or to supplement a basal reading program.
- For reading groups . . . to provide skills practice at the appropriate levels.
- For individual use . . . to help build a completely individualized program.
- For at-home practice . . . to expand on skills learned in the classroom.

Send all inquiries to: McGraw-Hill Consumer Products, 8787 Orion Place, Columbus, OH 43240-4027

i

Index *of* Skills for *Reading Grade K*

Numerals indicate the exercise pages on which these skills appear.

Auditory Skills

Associate sounds with letters—17, 21, 22, 26, 33, 34, 39, 46, 47, 52, 59, 61, 65, 71, 73, 78, 84, 88,89, 90
Discriminate initial sounds—16, 20, 25, 32, 38, 45, 51,58, 64, 70, 77, 83, 89
Discriminate final sounds—88
Discriminate medial vowel sounds—27, 40, 60, 72, 85
Recognize rhyming words—55, 68

Visual Skills

Associate numerals with a set—11, 12
Discriminate colors—2, 3, 4, 5
Discriminate letters—15, 19, 24, 31, 37, 44, 50, 57, 63, 69, 76, 82, 87
Discriminate shapes—6, 7, 8, 9
Discriminate sight words—91, 92
Identify colors—4, 5, 7
Identify numerals 1 through 5—11
Identify numerals 6 through 10—12
Identify shapes—8, 9, 10
Recognize size relationships—43, 74, 75
Use left-to-right progression—2, 3, 6, 8, 9,10, 15, 16,17, 19, 20, 21, 22, 24, 25, 26, 27, 28, 31, 32, 33, 34, 37, 38, 39, 40, 41, 43, 44, 45, 46, 47, 49, 50, 51, 52, 56, 57, 58, 59, 60, 61, 63, 64, 65, 68, 69, 70, 71, 72, 73, 76, 77, 78, 79, 82, 83, 84, 85, 87, 88, 89, 90, 91, 92

Motor Skills

Complete shapes—10
Coordinate eye-hand movements—7, 10, 30, 55

Oral Language and Vocabulary Skills

Give descriptions—6, 7, 8, 9, 10, 18, 29, 62, 86
Identify objects—2, 3, 4, 5, 28, 38, 41, 43, 49, 55, 56, 68, 75
Relate personal experiences—18, 42, 54, 79
Tell a story—13, 14, 23, 35, 36, 48, 53, 62, 74, 79, 86
Use complete sentences—13, 14, 23, 35, 36, 48, 53, 62, 74, 79, 86

Comprehension Skills

Classify objects—28, 30, 35, 41, 49, 54, 56, 62, 86
Determine the main idea—13, 14, 18, 23, 29, 35, 36, 42, 48, 53, 54, 62, 67, 74, 80, 86
Distinguish between reality and fantasy—54, 74
Draw conclusions—13, 18, 23, 29, 42, 48, 54, 62, 67, 74, 80, 86
Follow directions—*All exercise pages*
Locate facts and details—13, 18, 23, 29, 35, 42, 62, 67, 74, 80, 86
Make comparisons and contrasts—13, 18, 23, 29, 35, 62, 67, 74, 80, 86
Predict outcomes—13, 23, 48, 79
Recognize cause and effect relationships—13, 18, 23, 42, 79
Sequence events—14, 29, 36, 48, 53, 74
Understand directional terms—66, 81

Letters and Sounds

a—24, 25, 26, 27, 34
b—15,16,17,22
c—37, 38, 39, 47
d—63, 64, 65, 73
e—37, 38, 39, 40, 47
f—44, 45, 46, 47
g—57, 58, 59, 61
h—50, 51, 52, 61
i—57, 58, 59, 60, 61
j—63, 64, 65, 73
k—31, 32, 33, 34
l—44, 45, 46, 47
m—15, 16, 17, 22
n—19, 20, 21, 22
o—69, 70, 71, 72, 73
p—19, 20, 21, 22
q—76, 77, 78, 90
r—50, 51, 52, 61
s—24, 25, 26, 34
t—31, 32, 33, 34
u—82, 83, 84, 85, 90
v—76, 77, 78, 90
w—69, 70, 71, 73
x—87, 88
y—82, 83, 84, 90
z—87, 89

Working with Words

Blends

fl—134, 140	sl—122, 126	st—122, 126
pl—120, 126	sn—124, 140	tr—130, 140

Final consonants

n— 136, 141	p—132, 141	s—138, 141
k—136, 141	r—126, 141	t—128, 141
l—134, 141		

Initial consonants

b—90, 140	k—96, 116	t—100, 141
c—106, 141	l—92, 141	v—112, 120
d—94, 141	m—112, 141	w—94, 141
f—104, 118	n—102, 116	y—114, 120
g—114, 141	p—108, 118	z—106, 118
h—90, 116	r—98, 120	
j—102, 141	s—92, 141	

Short vowels

a—96, 104, 130, 132	o—110, 116, 124, 130, 138
e—100, 104, 124, 132, 138	u—118, 124, 132
i—108, 116, 130, 138	

Knowing the Words

Classification—98, 110, 128, 140
Sight Vocabulary—143, *All lessons*
Word Recognition—142, *All lessons*

Reading and Thinking

Context Clues—102, 114, 118, 124
Drawing Conclusions—104, 128, 136, 140
Facts and Details—94, 116, 126, 132
Picture Clues—92, 96, 100, 108, 112, 122
Predicting Outcomes—110, 130, 134, 138
Sequence—90, 98, 106, 120

Learning to Study

Following Directions—*All activity pages*

SPECTRUM READING
Grade K

Table of Contents

Which picture is different?

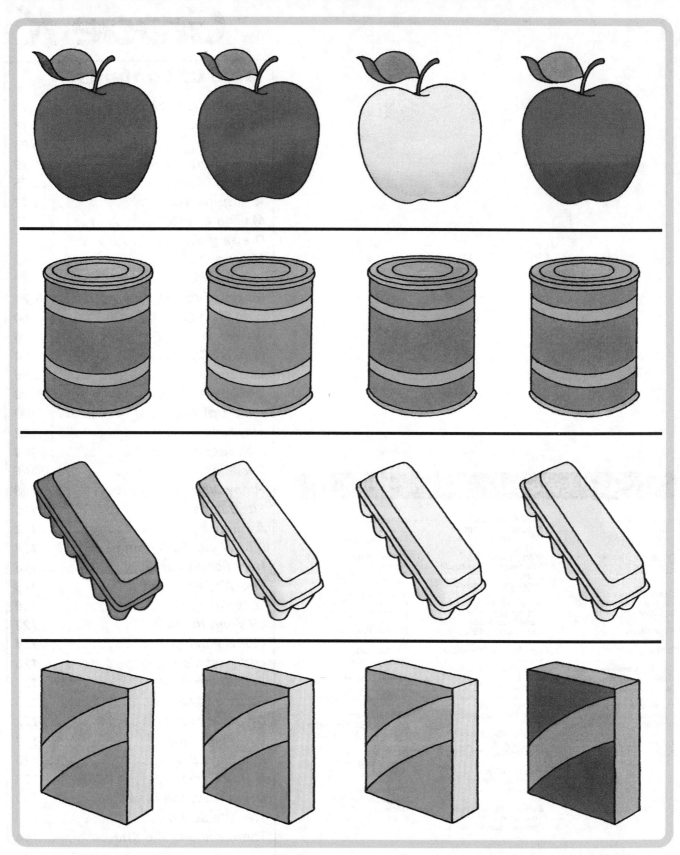

Directions: In each row, put an **X** on the object that is a color different from the others.

Home Practice: Point to an object in each row. Ask the child to name an object in the room that is the same color.

Find the Colors

Directions: Circle each object with the crayon that matches the color of the object.

Home Practice: Point to the pictures in left-to-right order and ask the child to name each object and its color.

5

Which shapes look alike?

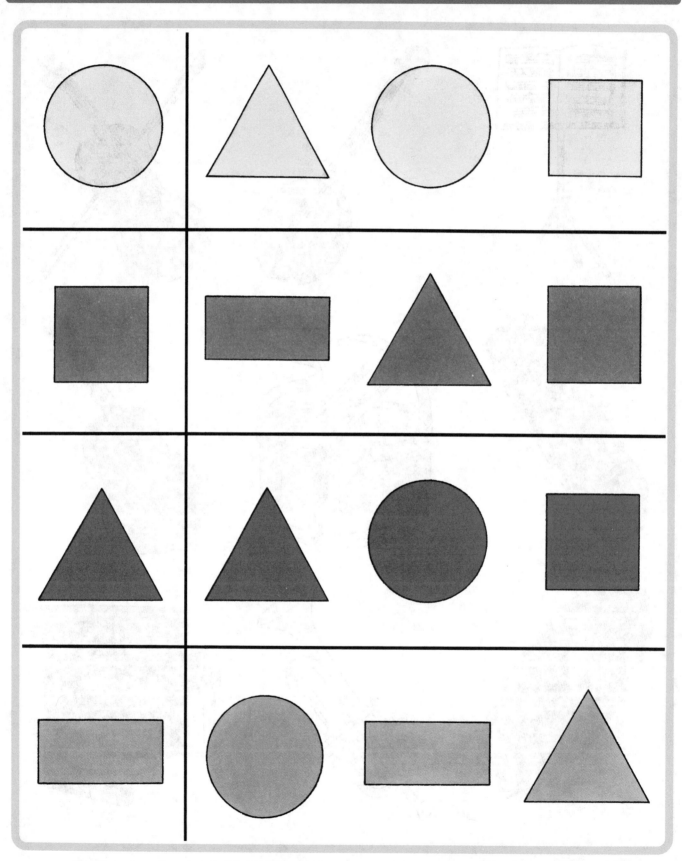

Directions: In each row, circle the shape that matches the first shape in that row.

Home Practice: Describe a shape on this page. Then have the child point to that shape.

Match the Shapes

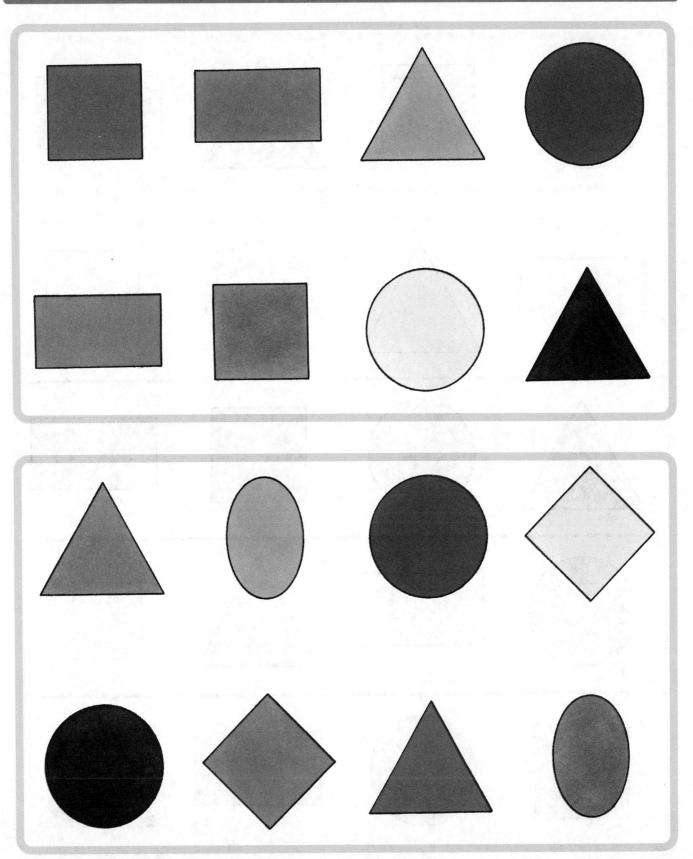

Directions: Draw a line to connect the shapes that match each other.

Home Practice: Point to shapes at random and have the child name the color.

7

Find the Shapes

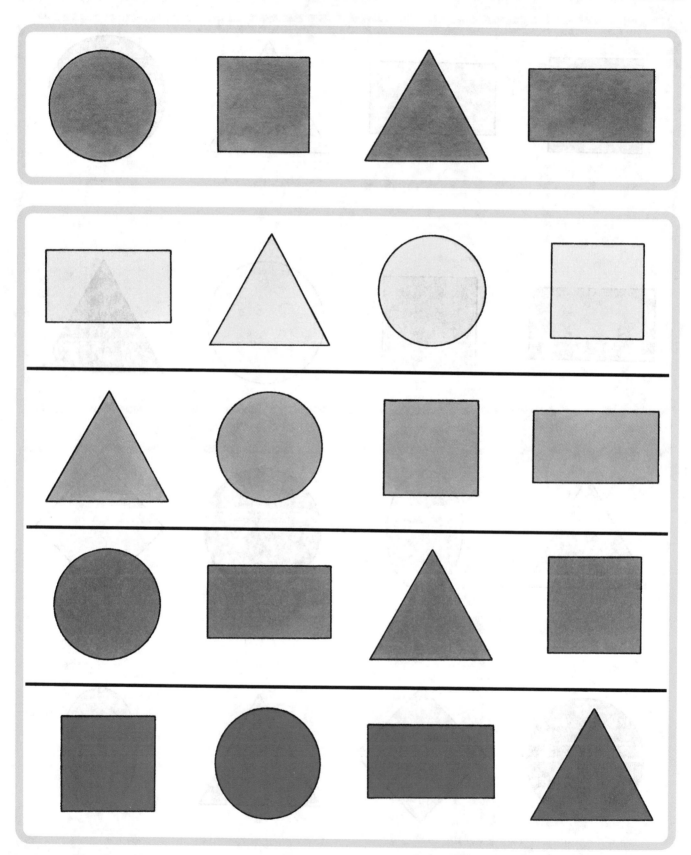

Directions: In each row, circle the shape you are told to circle.

Home Practice: Play a game by having the child point to a shape when you have described it. *(green square)*

Find the Shapes

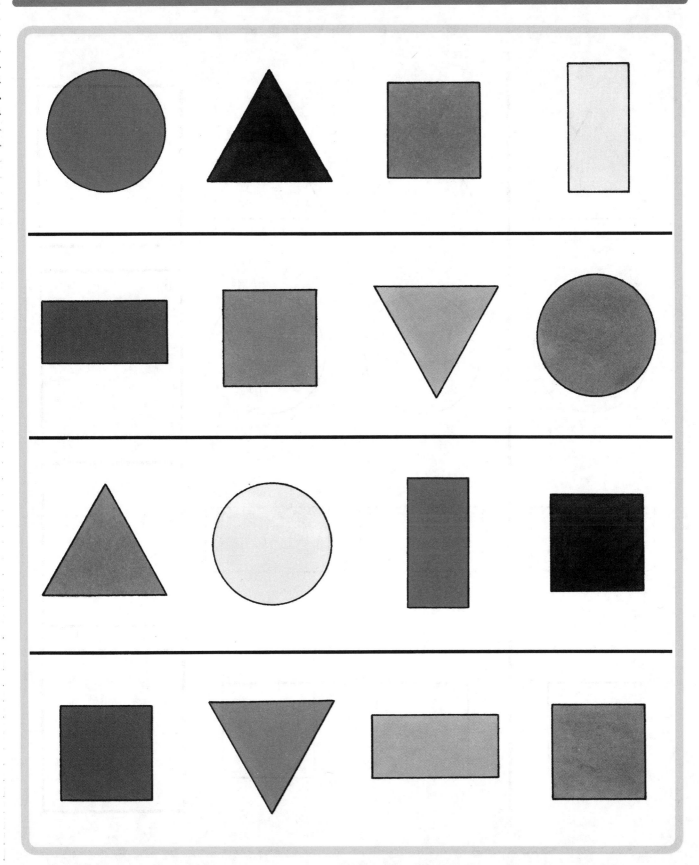

Directions: In each row, circle the shape that you are told to circle.

Home Practice: Play a game by pointing to shapes. Have the child name each one.

9

Finish the Shapes

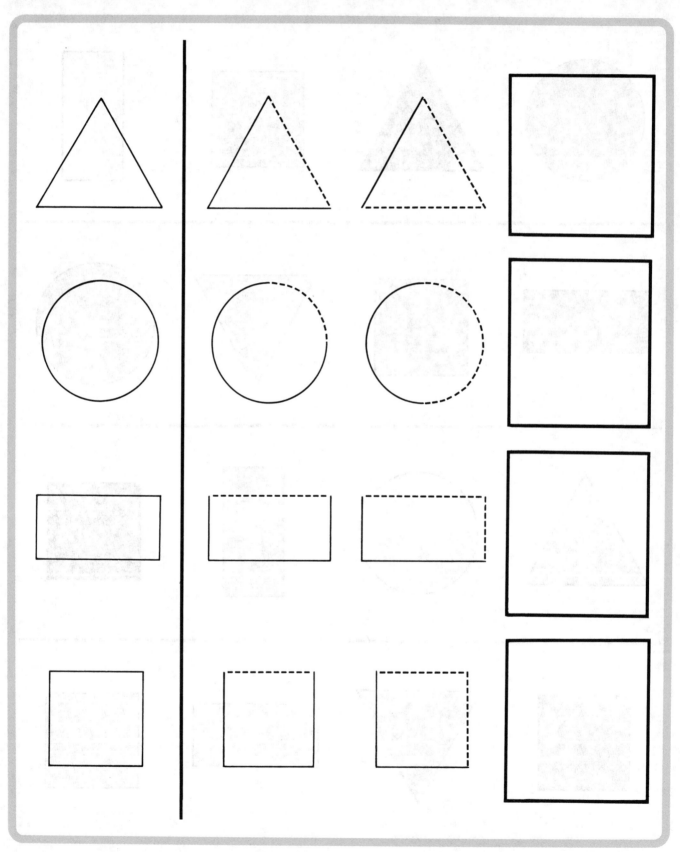

Directions: In each row, trace the dashed lines to complete the shapes. Then draw the same shape in the last box.

Home Practice: Play a game of review by pointing to a shape and having the child identify it.

How many are there?

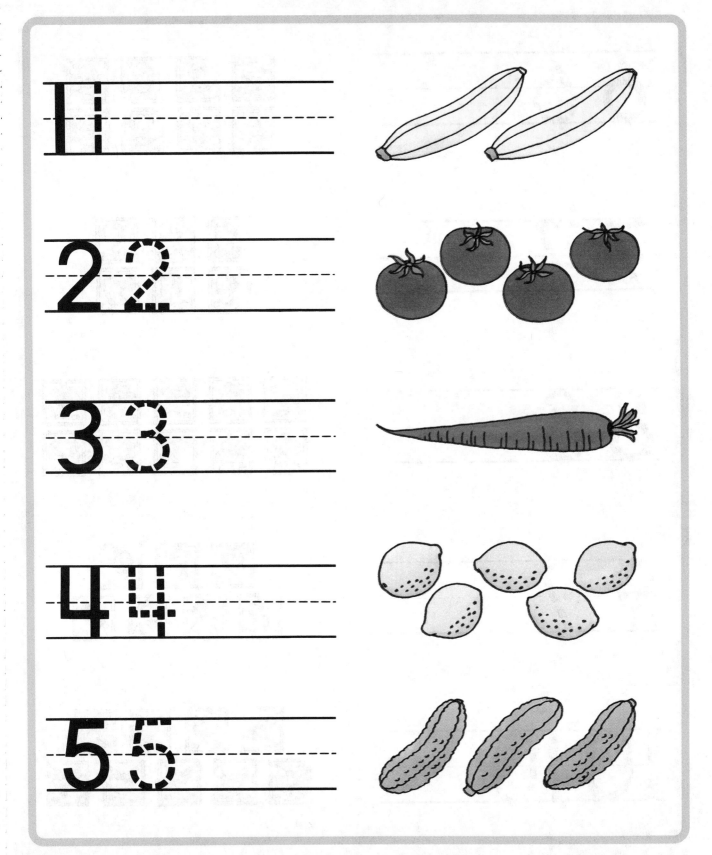

1

2 2

3 3

4 4

5 5

Directions: Trace each numeral and write it. Then draw a line from the numeral to the set it represents.

Home Practice: Ask the child to name the objects. Then have the child count each set of objects.

11

How many are there?

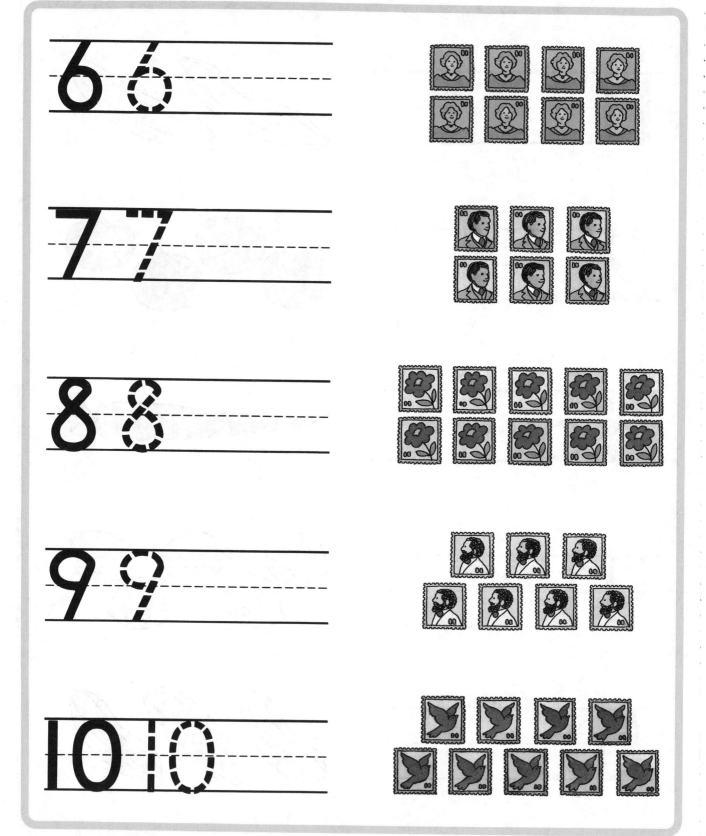

Directions: Trace each numeral and write it. Then draw a line from the numeral to the set it represents.

Home Practice: Ask the child to name the objects and tell what colors they are. Then have the child count each set of objects.

Shopping for Food

Directions: Discuss the picture.

Home Practice: Ask the child to look at the picture and describe what each person is doing.

13

What is the right order?

Directions: In the box, put a **1** under the picture that happened first, **2** under the picture that happened next, and **3** under the picture that happened last.

Home Practice: Have the child tell in correct sequence the story that is represented by each set of pictures.

Match the Letters

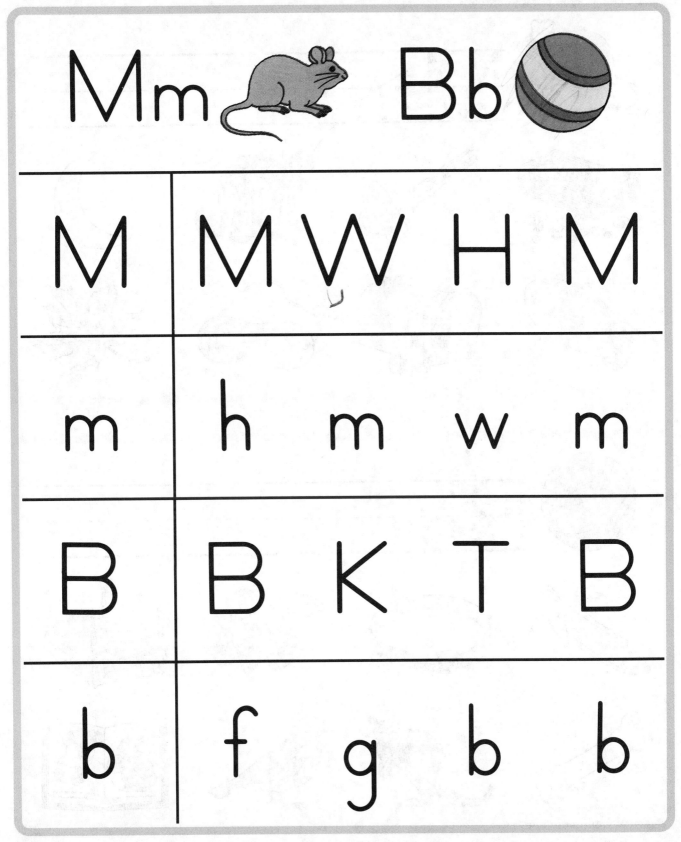

M m   B b

M	M	W	H	M
m	h	m	w	m
B	B	K	T	B
b	f	g	b	b

Directions: In each row, circle the letters that match the first letter in the row.

Home Practice: Point to a circled letter in each row. Ask the child to find and point to that letter in a magazine or newspaper.

15

Match the Sounds

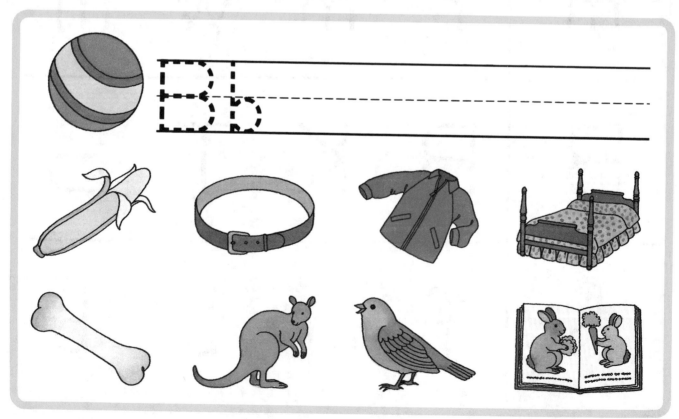

Directions: Name the pictures. Circle each picture whose name begins with the sound you hear at the beginning of *mouse*. Then do the same thing for *ball*.

Home Practice: Ask the child to name two circled pictures from each part of the page and then find objects in the room whose names begin with the same sound.

The Sounds of M and B

mouse

Mm

ball

Bb

Directions: Trace the letters and write them. Circle each picture whose name begins with **m** and write **m** on the line below it. Put an **X** on the pictures whose names do not begin with the sound of **m.** Then do the same for **b.**

Home Practice: Play a guessing game using the pictures. Make up clues such as this: *My name begins with the sound of m. I keep a hand warm. What am I? (mitten)*

17

At the Zoo

Directions: Discuss the picture.

Home Practice: Have the child name each animal and tell something special about it.

Match the Letters

N	V N N M
n	n m u n
P	B P P R
p	p q p j

Directions: In each row, circle the letters that match the first letter in the row.

Home Practice: Point to a circled letter in each row. Ask the child to find and point to that letter in a magazine or newspaper.

19

Match the Sounds

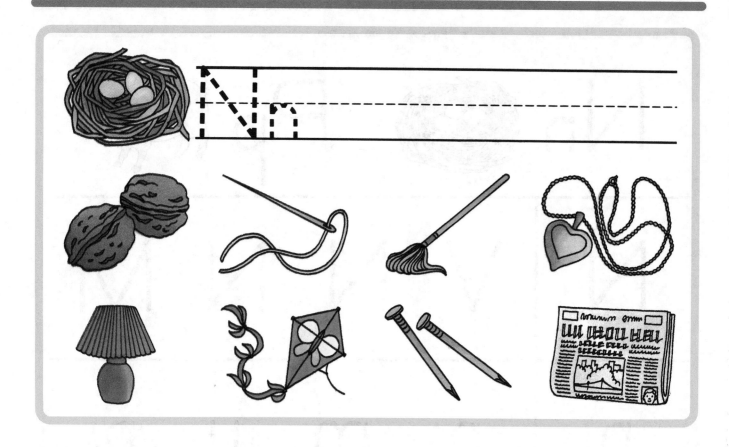

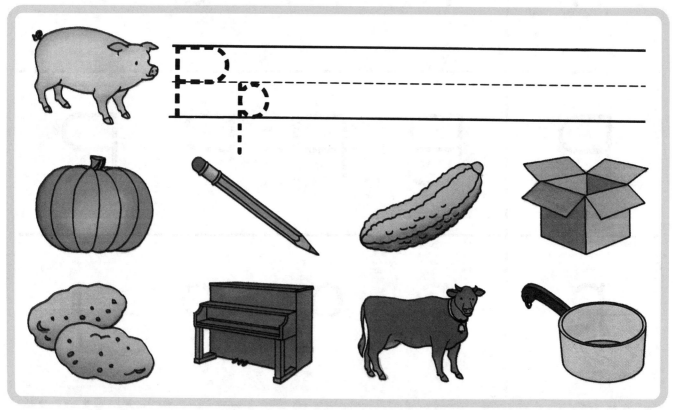

Directions: Name the pictures. Circle each picture whose name begins with the sound you hear at the beginning of *nest*. Then do the same thing for *pig*.

Home Practice: Ask the child to name two circled pictures from each part of the page and then find objects in the room whose names begin with the same sound.

The Sounds of N and P

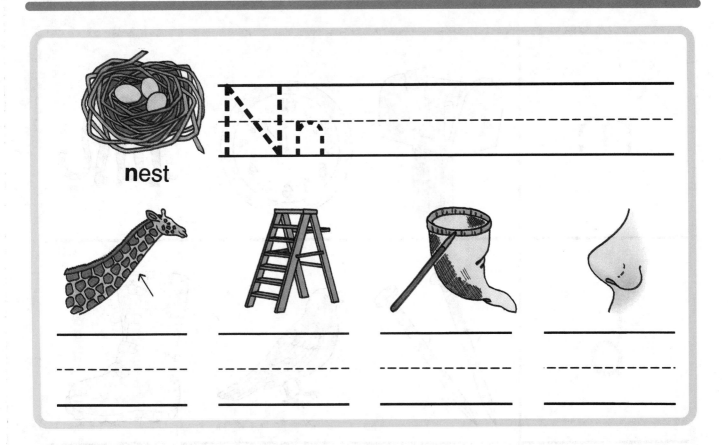

nest

pig

Directions: Trace the letters and write them. Circle each picture whose name begins with **n** and write **n** on the line below it. Put an **X** on the pictures whose names do not begin with **n.** Then do the same for **p.**

Home Practice: Play a guessing game using the pictures. Make up clues such as this: *My name begins with the sound of **n**. You smell with me. What am I? (nose)*

21

The Sounds of M, B, N, and P

Directions: Look at the letter at the beginning of each row. Circle each picture whose name begins with the sound of that letter.

Home Practice: Have the child point to and name all the animals on this page (*monkey, bird*) and all the things you wear (*boot, bow*). Then have the child say the letter that stands for the beginning sound of each name.

On a Farm

Directions: Discuss the pictures.

Home Practice: Ask the child to identify the activity of each person in the pictures.

23

Match the Letters

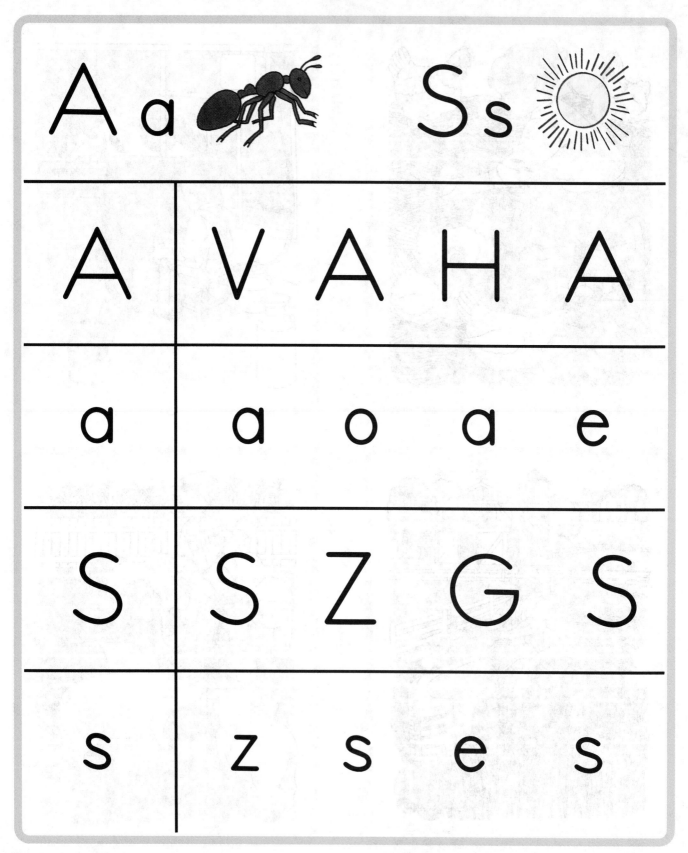

A a   S s

A	V A H A
a	a o a e
S	S Z G S
s	z s e s

Directions: In each row, circle the letters that match the first letter in the row.

Home Practice: Point to a circled letter in each row. Ask the child to find and point to that letter in a magazine or newspaper.

Match the Sounds

Directions: Name the pictures. Circle each picture whose name begins with the sound you hear at the beginning of *ant*. Then do the same thing for *sun*.

Home Practice: Ask the child to name two circled pictures from each part of the page and then find objects in the room whose names begin with the same sound.

The Sounds of A and S

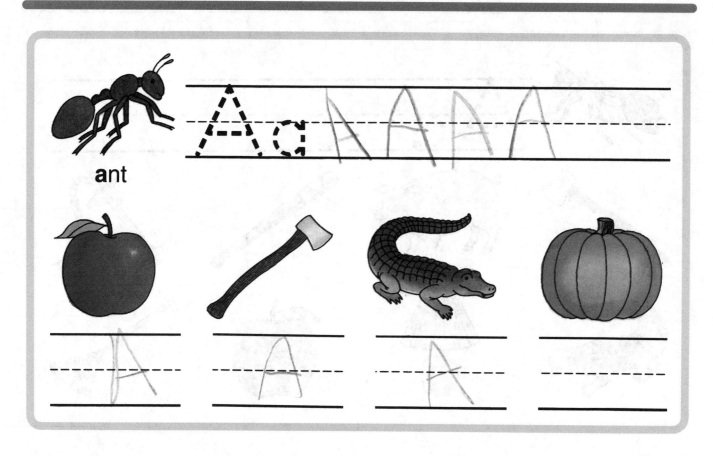

ant

sun

Directions: Trace the letters and write them. Circle each picture whose name begins with **a** and write **a** on the line below
it. Put an **X** on the pictures whose names do not begin with **a.**
Then do the same for **s.**

Home Practice: Play a guessing game using the pictures.
Make up clues such as this: *My name begins with the sound
of* **s.** *You cut wood with me. What am I? (saw)*

Match the Sound

hand

Directions: Name the pictures. Circle each picture whose name has the sound you hear in the middle of *hand*.

Home Practice: Ask the child to point to and name three circled pictures. Then say each of these words and have the child tell you whether it has the same middle sound as hand: *sad, hot, like, tan*.

27

Which belong together?

Directions: In each row, circle the three objects that belong together.

Home Practice: Have the child name the pictures in each row that are circled and then have him or her tell how the objects are alike.

Through the Year

Directions: Discuss the pictures.

Home Practice: Have the child compare the children's clothing and the appearance of the outdoors in these pictures.

29

Which belong together?

Directions: Draw a line from each object in the first row to an object that goes with it in the next row. Do the same thing for the third and fourth rows.

Home Practice: Have the child tell you how the objects that go together are related.

Match the Letters

K k	T t

K	K	N	R	K
k	k	l	k	t
T	T	L	T	Y
t	h	t	t	l

Directions: In each row, circle the letters that match the first letter in the row.

Home Practice: Point to a circled letter in each row. Ask the child to find and point to that letter in a magazine or newspaper.

31

Match the Sounds

Directions: Name the pictures. Circle each picture whose name begins with the sound you hear at the beginning of *kite*. Then do the same thing for *tent*.

Home Practice: Ask the child to name two circled pictures from each part of the page and then find objects in the room whose names begin with the same sound.

The Sounds of K and T

kite

tent

Directions: Trace the letters and write them. Circle each picture whose name begins with **k** and write **k** on the line below it. Put an **X** on the pictures whose names do not begin with **k**. Then do the same for **t**.

Home Practice: Play a guessing game using the pictures. Make up clues such as this: *My name begins with the sound of k. I can open a door. What am I? (key)*

33

The Sounds of A, S, K, and T

Directions: Look at the letter at the beginning of each row. Circle each picture whose name begins with the sound of that letter.

Home Practice: Have the child point to and name all the animals on this page. *(alligator, seal, turkey, turtle)* Then have the child say the letter that stands for the beginning sound of each animal name.

Making Music

Directions: Discuss the picture.

Home Practice: Ask the child to look at the picture and describe what each person is doing.

35

What is the right order?

Directions: In the box, put a **1** under the picture that happened first, **2** under the picture that happened next, and **3** under the picture that happened last.

Home Practice: Have the child tell in correct sequence the story that is represented by each set of pictures.

Match the Letters

C	C G C O
c	o c n c
E	E F B E
e	a e v e

Directions: In each row, circle the letters that match the first letter in the row.

Home Practice: Point to a circled letter in each row. Ask the child to find and point to that letter in a magazine or newspaper.

37

Match the Sounds

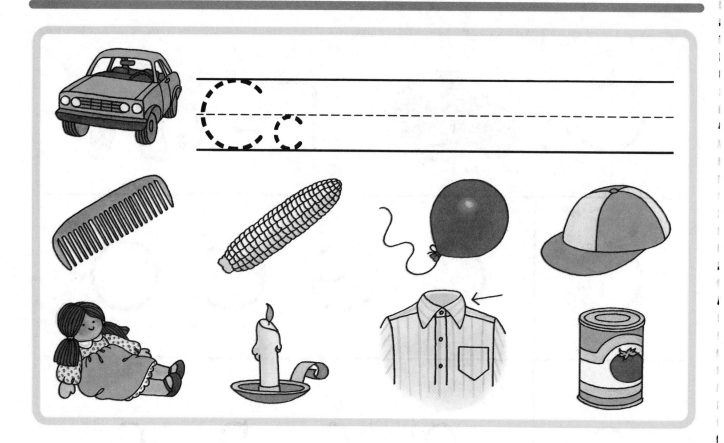

Directions: Name the pictures. Circle each picture whose name begins with the sound you hear at the beginning of *car.* Then do the same thing for *elephant.*

Home Practice: Ask the child to name two circled pictures from each part of the page and then find objects in the room whose names begin with the same sound.

The Sounds of C and E

car

elephant

39

Directions: Trace the letters and write them. Circle each picture whose name begins with **c** and write **c** on the line below it. Put an **X** on the pictures whose names do not begin with **c**. Then do the same for **e**.

Home Practice: Play a guessing game using the pictures. Make up clues such as this: *My name begins with the sound of c. I give you milk. What am I? (cow)*

Match the Sound

fence

Directions: Name the pictures. Circle each picture whose name has the sound you hear in the middle of *fence*.

Home Practice: Ask the child to point to and name three circled pictures. Then say each of these words and have the child tell you whether it has the same middle sound as *fence*: *box, pen, bike, web*.

Which belong together?

Directions: In each row, circle the three objects that belong together.

Home Practice: Have the child name the pictures in each row that are circled and then have him or her tell how the objects are alike.

41

A Hospital Stay

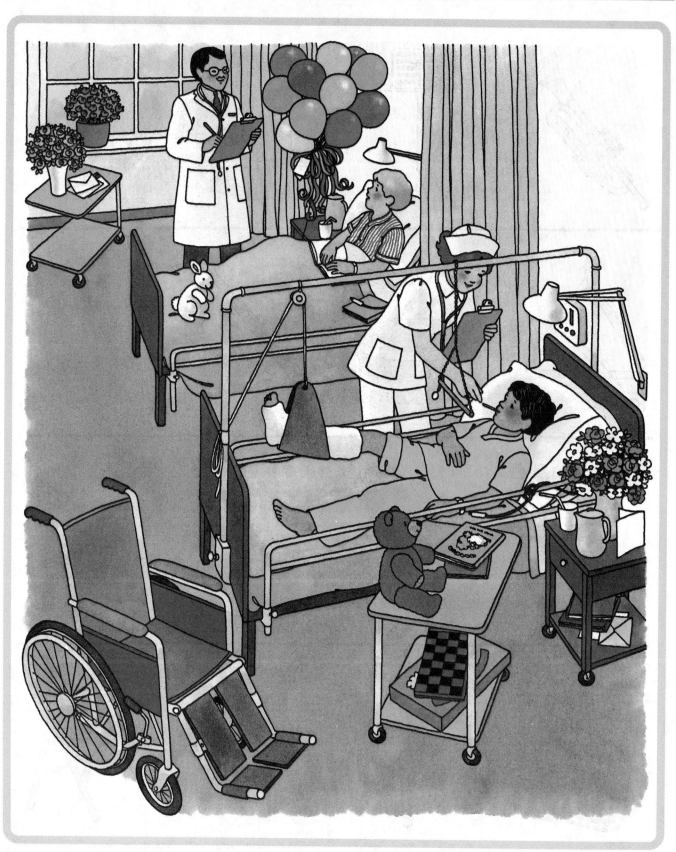

Directions: Discuss the picture.

Home Practice: Ask the child to tell what each person in this picture might be thinking or saying.

Look at the Sizes

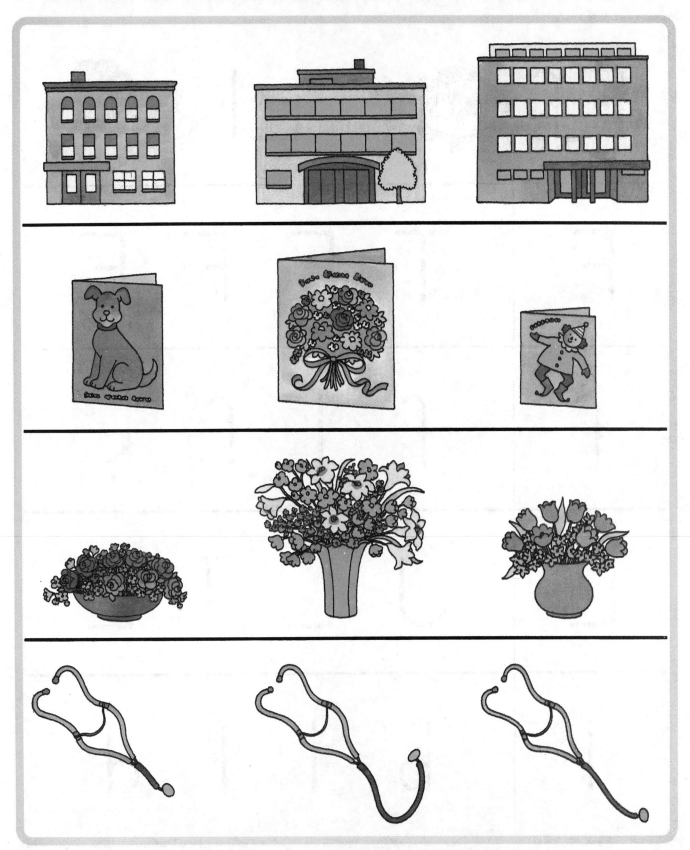

Directions: In each row, circle the object that you are told to circle.

Home Practice: Ask the child about the sizes of the objects in each row by using questions such as this: *Which building is biggest?*

43

Match the Letters

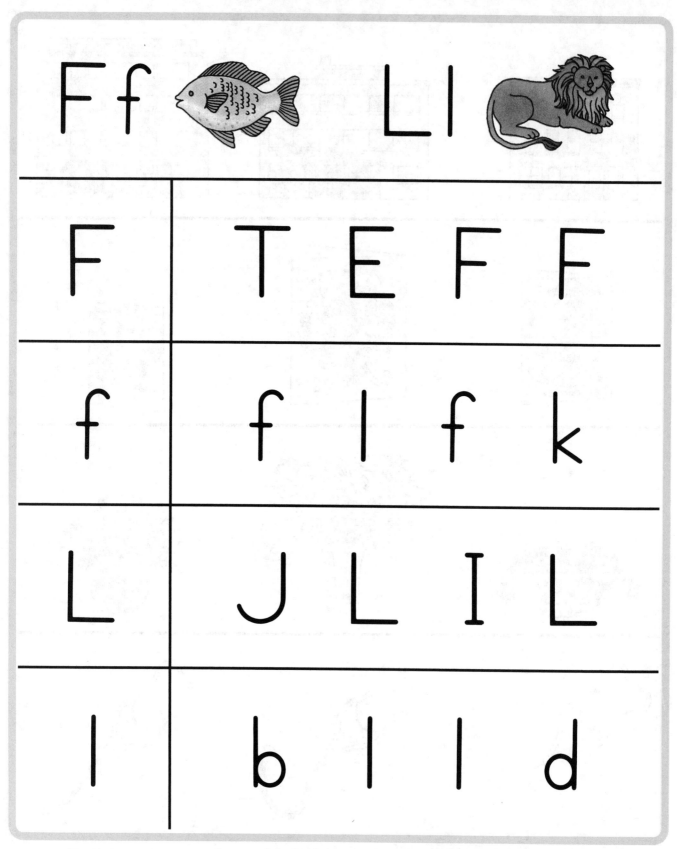

F f 🐟	L l 🦁
F	T E F F
f	f l f k
L	J L I L
l	b l l d

Directions: In each row, circle the letters that match the first letter in the row.

Home Practice: Point to a circled letter in each row. Ask the child to find and point to that letter in a magazine or newspaper.

Match the Sounds

Directions: Name the pictures. Circle each picture whose name begins with the sound you hear at the beginning of *fish*. Then do the same thing for *lion*.

Home Practice: Ask the child to name two circled pictures from each part of the page and then find objects in the room whose names begin with the same sound.

45

The Sounds of F and L

fish

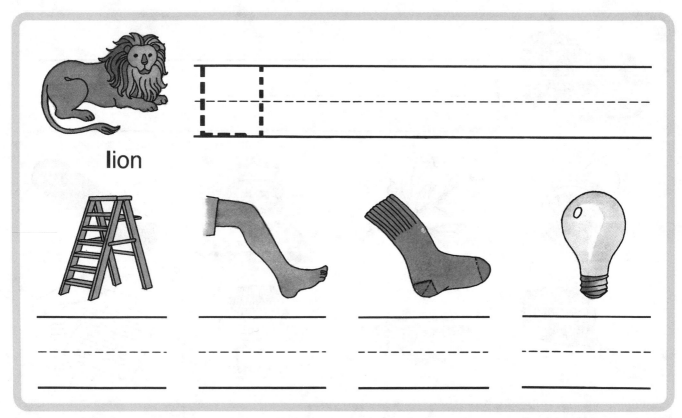

lion

Directions: Trace the letters and write them. Circle each picture whose name begins with **f** and write **f** on the line below it. Put an **X** on the pictures whose names do not begin with the sound of **f.** Then do the same for **l.**

Home Practice: Play a guessing game using the pictures. Make up clues such as this: *My name begins with the sound of l. You climb up me. What am I? (ladder)*

The Sounds of C, E, F, and L

Directions: Look at the letter at the beginning of each row. Circle each picture whose name begins with the sound of that letter.

Home Practice: Have the child point to and name all the objects that can be played (*drum, piano*) or with which a child can play (*football, doll*). Then have the child say the letter that stands for the beginning sound of each name.

47

Mailing a Letter

Directions: Discuss the pictures.

Home Practice: Ask the child to look at the pictures and describe what each person is doing.

Which belong together?

Directions: In each row, circle the picture that belongs with the first picture in the row.

Home Practice: Have the child tell you how the objects that go together are related.

49

Match the Letters

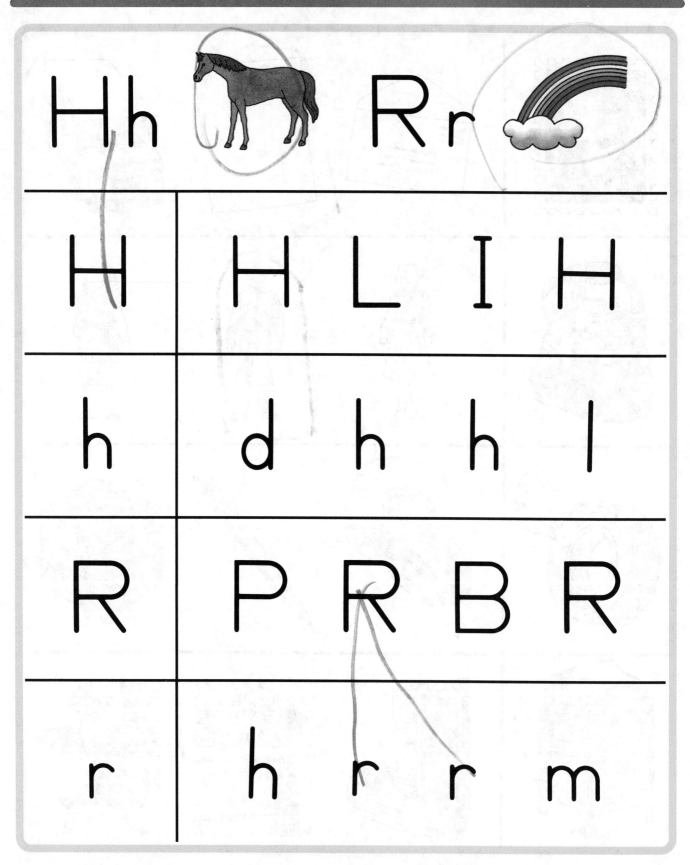

Hh	Rr
H	H L I H
h	d h h l
R	P R B R
r	h r m

Directions: In each row, circle the letters that match the first letter in the row.

Home Practice: Point to a circled letter in each row. Ask the child to find and point to that letter in a magazine or newspaper.

Match the Sounds

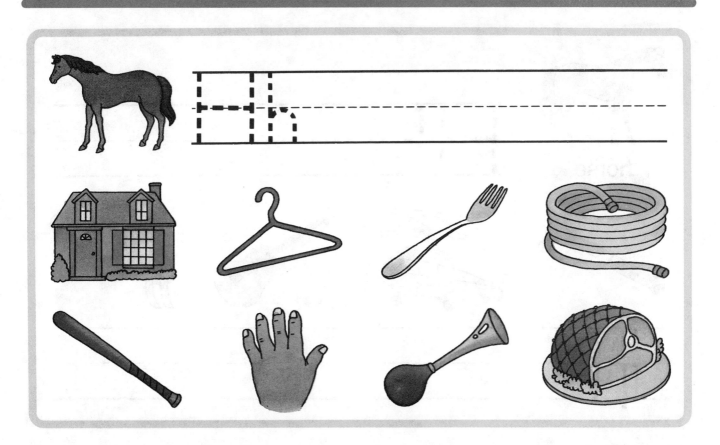

Directions: Name the pictures. Circle each picture whose name begins with the sound you hear at the beginning of *horse.* Then do the same thing for *rainbow.*

Home Practice: Ask the child to name two circled pictures from each part of the page and then find objects in the room whose names begin with the same sound.

The Sounds of H and R

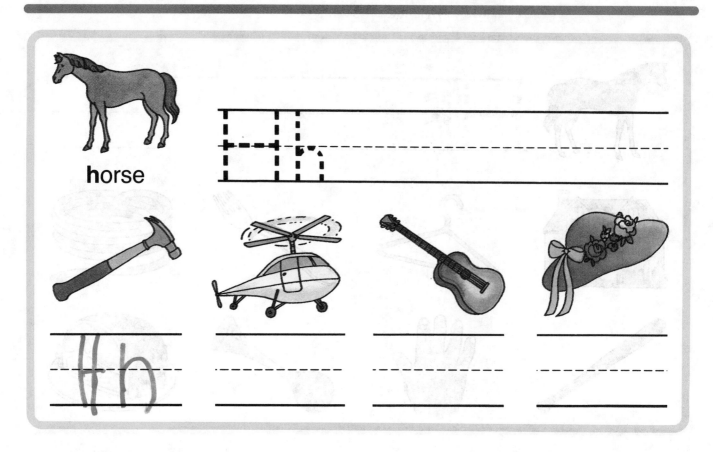

horse

rainbow

Directions: Trace the letters and write them. Circle each picture whose name begins with **h** and write **h** on the line below it. Put an **X** on the pictures whose names do not begin with **h**. Then do the same for **r**.

Home Practice: Play a guessing game using the pictures. Make up clues such as this: *My name begins with the sound of h. You pound with me. What am I? (hammer)*

What is the right order?

L **2**   S **3**   R **1**

M **3**   G **2**   S **1**

Directions: In the box, put a **1** under the picture that happened first, **2** under the picture that happened next, and **3** under the picture that happened last.

Home Practice: Have the child tell in correct sequence the story that is represented by each set of pictures.

53

Dressing Up

Directions: Discuss the picture.

Home Practice: Have the child name some of the objects found in this attic. Encourage the child to tell what the boy and girl in the picture might be thinking.

Match the Ones That Rhyme

Directions: Draw a line from each object in the first row to an object that rhymes with it in the next row. Do the same with rows three and four.

Home Practice: Say a word that rhymes with one of the picture names. Have the child point to the correct picture or pictures. Use clues such as this: *Find a picture with a name that rhymes with cat.* (hat, bat)

Which belong together?

Directions: Circle the three pictures in each row that belong together.

Home Practice: Have the child tell you how the circled pictures in each row are related.

Match the Letters

I i	G g
I	I H T I
i	i r i t
G	C O G
g	g y g j

Directions: In each row, circle the letters that match the first letter in the row.

Home Practice: Point to a circled letter in each row. Ask the child to find and point to that letter in a magazine or newspaper.

57

Match the Sounds

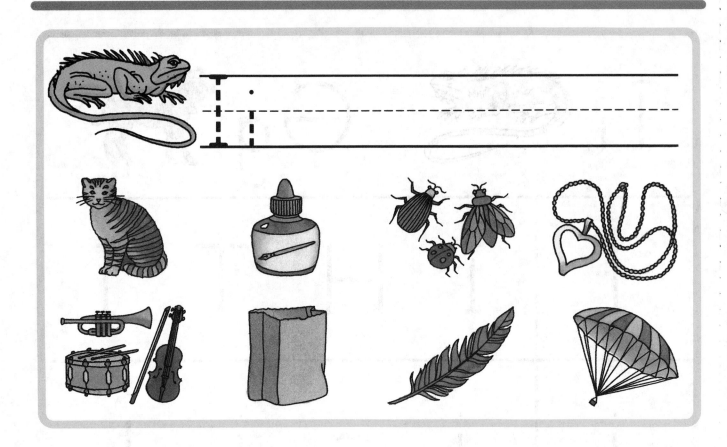

I i

G g

58 **Directions:** Name the pictures. Then circle each picture whose name begins with the sound you hear at the beginning of *iguana*. Then do the same thing for *goat*.

Home Practice: Ask the child to name two circled pictures from each part of the page and then find objects in the room whose names begin with the same sound.

The Sounds of I and G

iguana

goat

Directions: Trace the letters and write them. Circle each picture whose name begins with **i** and write **i** on the line below it. Put an **X** on the pictures whose names do not begin with **i**. Then do the same for **g**.

Home Practice: Play a guessing game using the pictures. Make up clues such as this: *My name begins with the sound of i. You find me in a pen. What am I? (ink)*

Match the Sound

chick

Directions: Name the pictures. Circle each picture whose name has the sound you hear in the middle of *chick*.

Home Practice: Ask the child to point to and name three circled pictures. Then say each of these words and have the child tell you whether it has the same middle sound as *chick*: *make, sit, sock, bib.*

The Sounds of H, R, I, and G

Directions: Look at the letter at the beginning of each row. Circle each picture whose name begins with the sound of that letter.

Home Practice: Have the child point to and name all the animals on this page. (*mouse, rooster, insects, goose*) Then have the child say the letter that stands for the beginning sound of each animal name.

61

Moving In

Directions: Discuss the picture.

Home Practice: Ask the child to look at the picture and tell what each person is doing and what he or she might be thinking.

Match the Letters

D d		**J j**		
D	O	D	D	B
d	d	h	g	d
J	U	J	L	J
j	j	p	j	q

Directions: In each row, circle the letters that match the first letter in the row.

Home Practice: Point to a circled letter in each row. Ask the child to find and point to that letter in a magazine or news-paper.

63

Match the Sounds

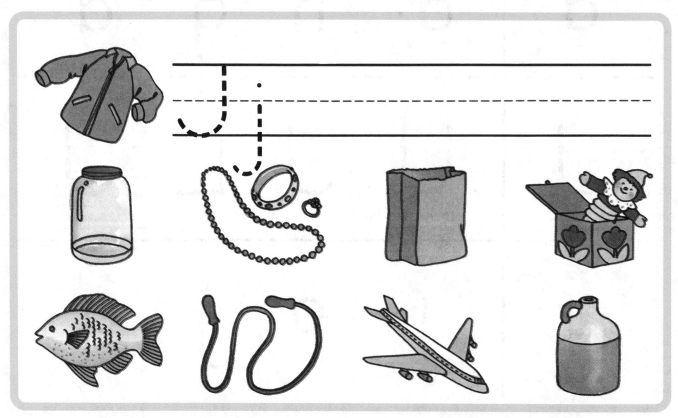

Directions: Name the pictures. Circle each picture whose name begins with the sound you hear at the beginning of *dog*. Then do the same thing for *jacket*.

Home Practice: Ask the child to name two circled pictures from each part of the page and then find objects in the room whose names begin with the same sound.

The Sounds of D and J

dog

jacket

Directions: Trace the letters and write them. Circle each picture whose name begins with **d** and write **d** on the line below it. Put an **X** on the pictures whose names do not begin with **d**. Then do the same for **j**.

Home Practice: Play a guessing game using the pictures. Make up clues such as this: *My name begins with the sound of j. You wear me to keep warm. What am I? (jacket)*

65

Where are they?

Directions: Circle each picture that you are told to circle.

Home Practice: Point to pictures at random and have the child describe them.

Visiting the Fire Station

Directions: Discuss the picture.

Home Practice: Ask the child to look at the picture and tell what each person might be thinking or saying.

Which ones rhyme?

Directions: In each row, circle a picture whose name rhymes with the first picture in the row.

Home Practice: Say a word that rhymes with one of the picture names. Have the child point to the correct picture or pictures. Use clues such as this: *Find a picture with a name that rhymes with cat. (hat)*

Match the Letters

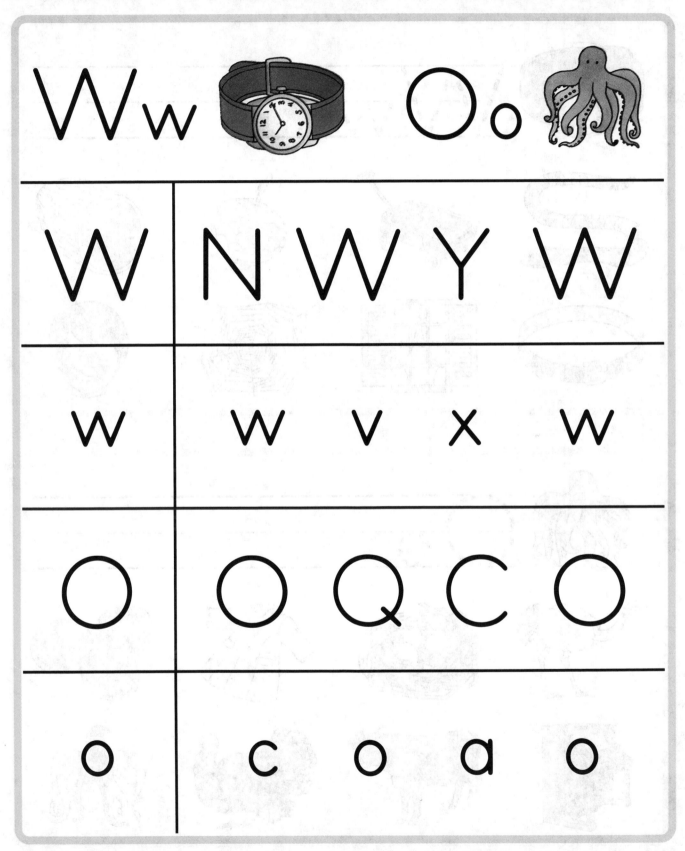

W w   O o

W	N W Y W
w	w v x w
O	O Q C O
o	c o a o

Directions: In each row, circle the letters that match the first letter in the row.

Home Practice: Point to a circled letter in each row. Ask the child to find and point to that letter in a magazine or newspaper.

Match the Sounds

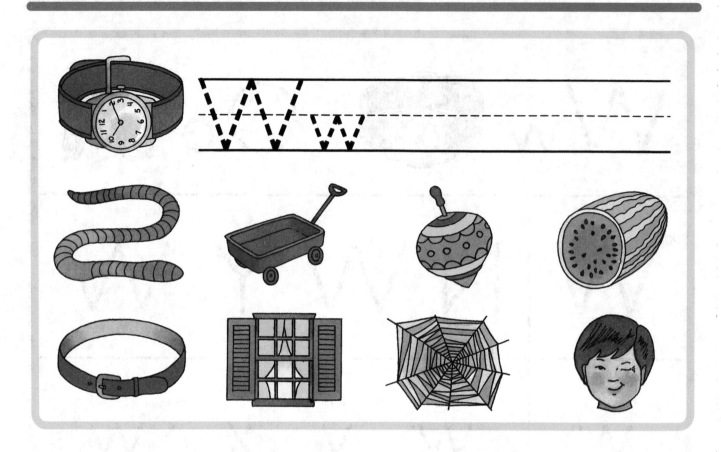

Directions: Name the pictures. Then circle each picture whose name begins with the sound you hear at the beginning of *watch.* Then do the same thing for *octopus.*

Home Practice: Ask the child to name two circled pictures from each part of the page and then find objects in the room whose names begin with the same sound.

The Sounds of W and O

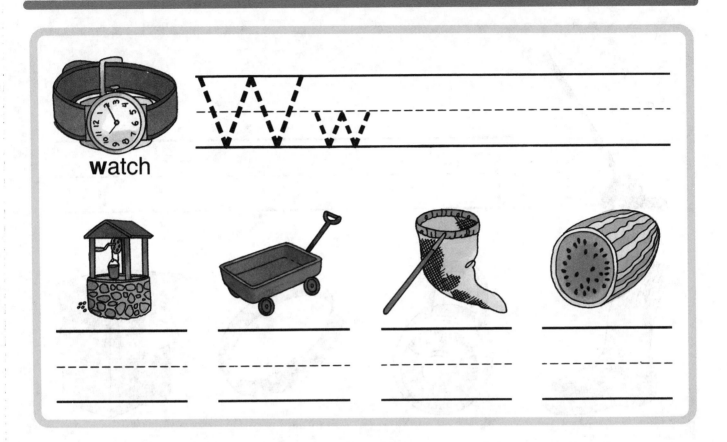

watch

octopus

Directions: Trace the letters and write them. Circle each picture whose name begins with **w** and write **w** on the line below it. Put an **X** on the pictures whose names do not begin with **w.** Then do the same for **o.**

Home Practice: Play a guessing game using the pictures. Make up clues such as this: *My name begins with the sound of w. I tell you the time. What am I? (watch)*

71

Match the Sound

mop

Directions: Name the pictures. Circle each picture whose name has the sound you hear in the middle of *mop*.

Home Practice: Ask the child to point to and name three circled pictures. Then say each of these words and have the child tell you whether it has the same middle sound as mop: *hot, red, take, box.*

The Sounds of D, J, W, and O

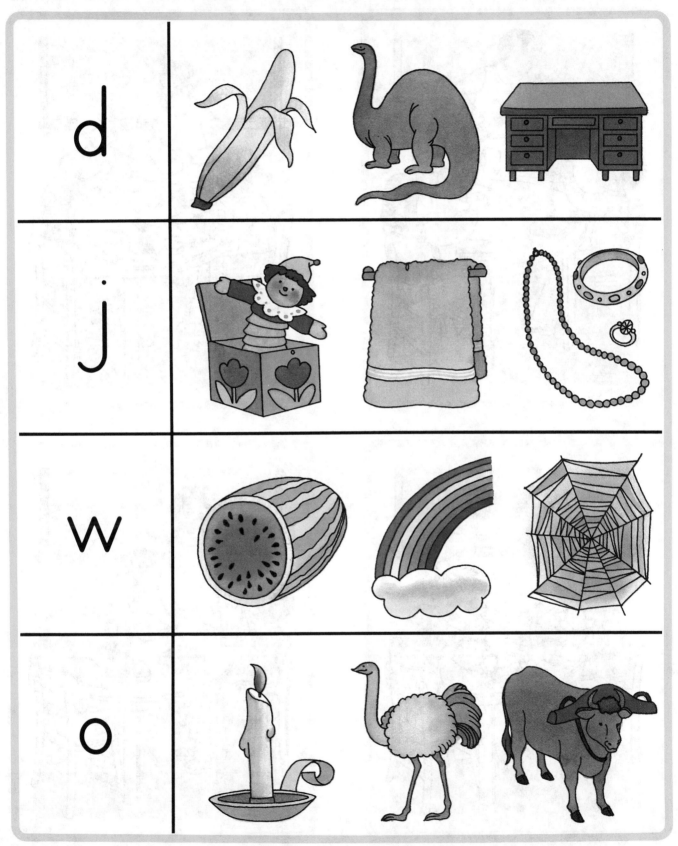

Directions: Look at the letter at the beginning of each row. Circle each picture whose name begins with the sound of that letter.

Home Practice: Have the child point to and name all the things to eat on this page (*banana, watermelon*) and all the animals (*dinosaur, ostrich, ox*). Then have the child say the letter that stands for the beginning sound of each name.

73

Making Puppets

Directions: Discuss the pictures.

Home Practice: Ask the child to look at the pictures and tell what each person is doing.

Look at the Sizes

Directions: In each row, circle the picture that you are told to circle.

Home Practice: Point to two puppets in the same row and tell ways they are alike and ways they are different.

Match the Letters

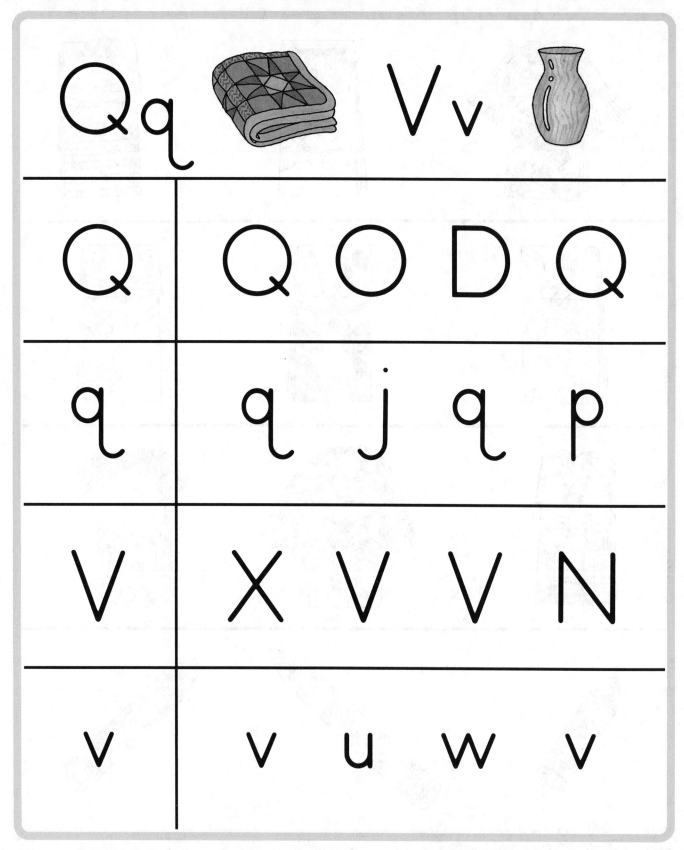

Q	Q O D Q
q	q j q p
V	X V V N
v	v u w v

Directions: In each row, circle the letters that match the first letter in the row.

Home Practice: Point to a circled letter in each row. Ask the child to find and point to that letter in a magazine or newspaper.

Match the Sounds

Directions: Name the pictures. Then circle each picture whose name begins with the sound you hear at the beginning of *quilt*. Then do the same thing for *vase*.

Home Practice: Ask the child to name two circled pictures from each part of the page and then find objects in the room whose names begin with the same sound.

77

The Sounds of Q and V

quilt

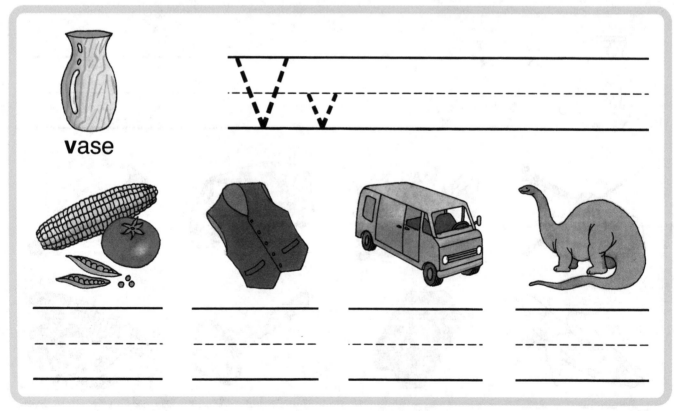

vase

Directions: Trace the letters and write them. Circle each picture whose name begins with **q** and write **q** on the line below it. Put an **X** on the pictures whose names do not begin with **q**. Then do the same for **v**.

Home Practice: Play a guessing game using the pictures. Make up clues such as this: *My name begins with the sound of q. I wear a crown on my head. Who am I? (queen)*

How will it look?

Directions: In each row, circle the picture that shows how the bag or table would look as a result of the first picture.

Home Practice: Point to a picture at random and ask the child to describe it.

79

Gym Class

Directions: Discuss the picture.

Home Practice: Ask the child to look at the picture and describe what each person is doing.

Where are they?

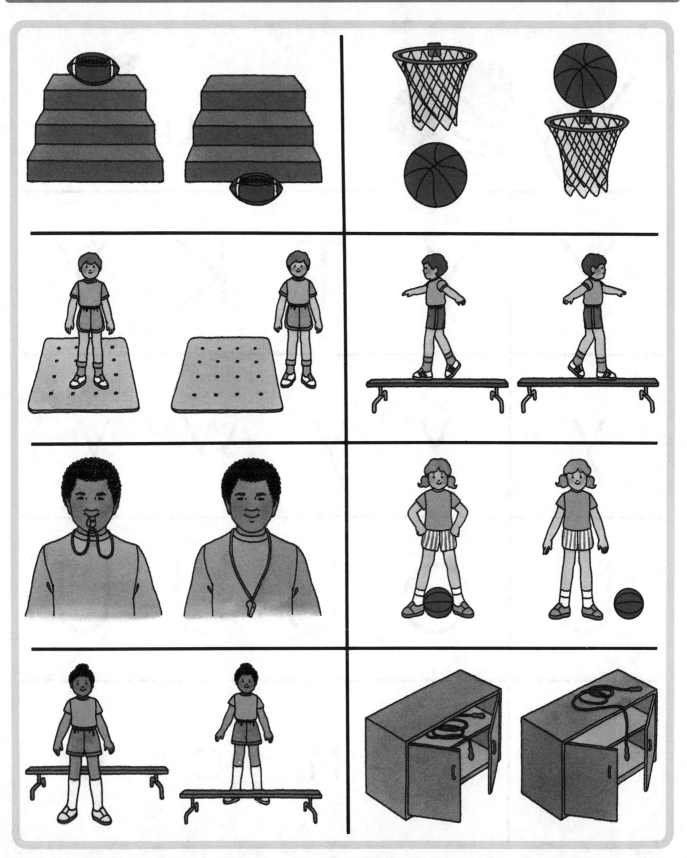

Directions: Circle each picture that you are told to circle.

Home Practice: Point to pictures at random and have the child describe them.

Match the Letters

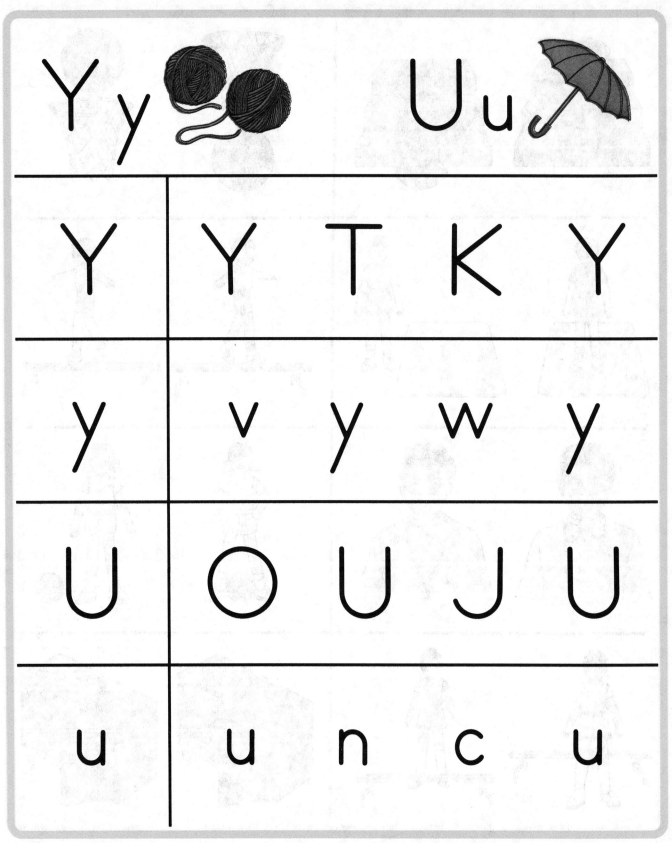

Y	Y	T	K	Y
y	v	y	w	y
U	O	U	J	U
u	u	n	c	u

Directions: In each row, circle the letters that match the first letter in the row.

Home Practice: Point to a circled letter in each row. Ask the child to find and point to that letter in a magazine or newspaper.

Match the Sounds

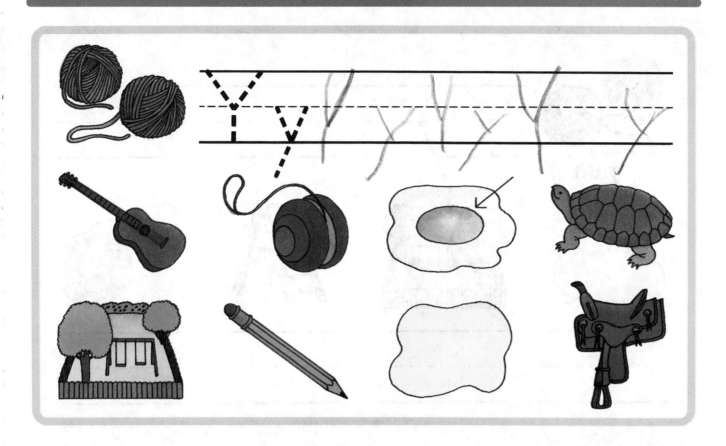

Directions: Name the pictures. Then circle each picture whose name begins with the sound you hear at the beginning of *yarn*. Then do the same thing for *umbrella*.

Home Practice: Ask the child to name two circled pictures from each part of the page and then find objects in the room whose names begin with the same sound.

83

The Sounds of Y and U

yarn

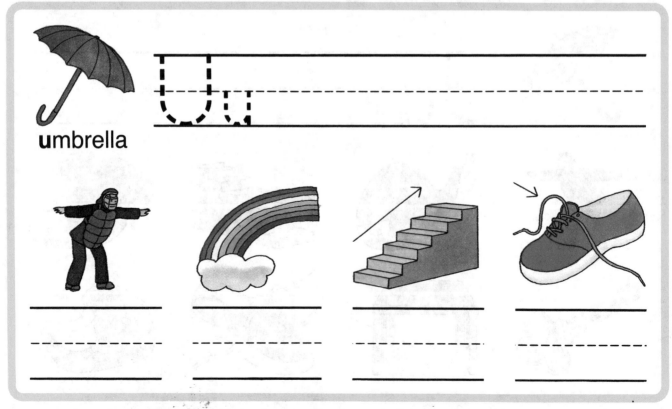

umbrella

84

Directions: Trace the letters and write them. Circle each picture whose name begins with **y** and write **y** on the line below it. Put an **X** on the pictures whose names do not begin with **y**. Then do the same for **u**.

Home Practice: Play a guessing game using the pictures. Make up clues such as this: *My name begins with the sound of y. You can play in me. What am I? (yard)*

Match the Sound

duck

Directions: Name the pictures. Circle each picture whose name has the sound you hear in the middle of *duck*.

Home Practice: Ask the child to point to and name three circled pictures. Then say each of these words and have the child tell you whether it has the same middle sound as *duck*: *cup, cake, bus, pet*.

85

A Pet Show

Directions: Discuss the picture.

Home Practice: Point to a pet at random and ask the child to name it and tell you something special about it.

Match the Letters

X x   Z z

X	Z	X	Y	X

x	y	x	z	x

Z	Z	N	S	Z

z	z	s	w	z

The Sound of X

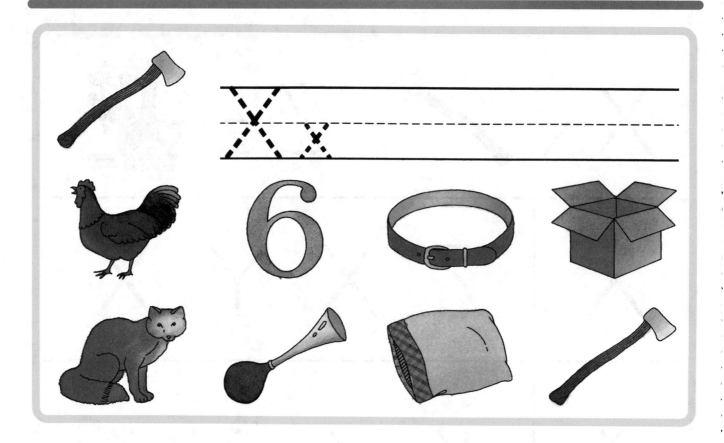

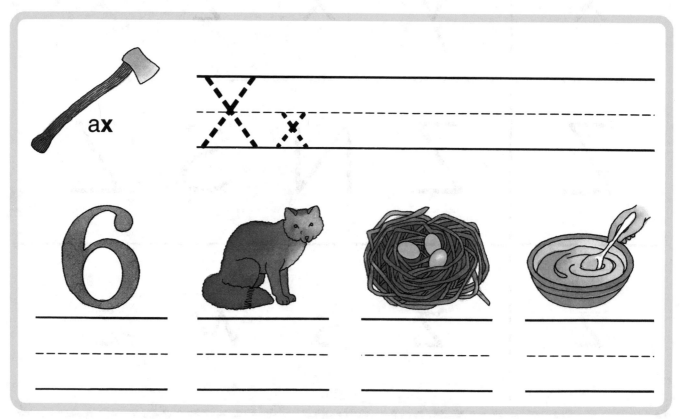

ax

88

Directions: *(Top)* Name the pictures. Then circle each picture whose name ends with the sound you hear at the end of *ax.* *(Bottom)* Circle each picture whose name ends with **x** and write **x** on the line below it. Trace the letters and write them.

Home Practice: Ask the child to name two circled pictures from each part of the page and then think of objects whose names end with the same sound.

The Sound of Z

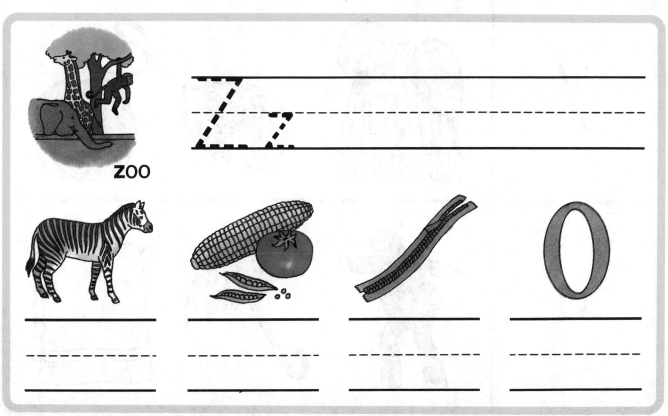

ZOO

Directions: *(Top)* Name the pictures. Circle each picture whose name begins with the sound you hear at the beginning of *zoo*. *(Bottom)* Circle each picture whose name begins with **z**. Write **z** on the line below it. Trace the letters and write them.

Home Practice: Play a guessing game using the pictures. Make up clues such as this: *My name begins with the sound of z. I am a striped animal. What am I? (zebra)*

The Sounds of Q, V, Y, and U

q

v

y

u

Directions: Look at the letter at the beginning of each row. Circle each picture whose name begins with the sound of that letter.

Home Practice: Have the child point to and name all the things to eat (*banana, watermelon*) or wear (*dress, vest*) on this page. Then have the child say the letter that stands for the beginning sound of each name.

Which words look alike?

cat	ball	cat	cat
ball	ball	tree	ball
dog	girl	dog	dog
tree	tree	dog	tree
girl	dog	girl	girl

Directions: In each row, circle the words that match the first word.

Home Practice: Point to any two words on the page and ask the child if they match.

91

Which words look alike?

Can	Can	See	Can
you	you	cat	you
see	the	see	see
the	can	the	the
cat	see	cat	cat

Can you see the cat?

Directions: In each row, circle the words that match the first word.

Home Practice: Point to any two words on the page and ask the child if they are alike or different.

My ABCs

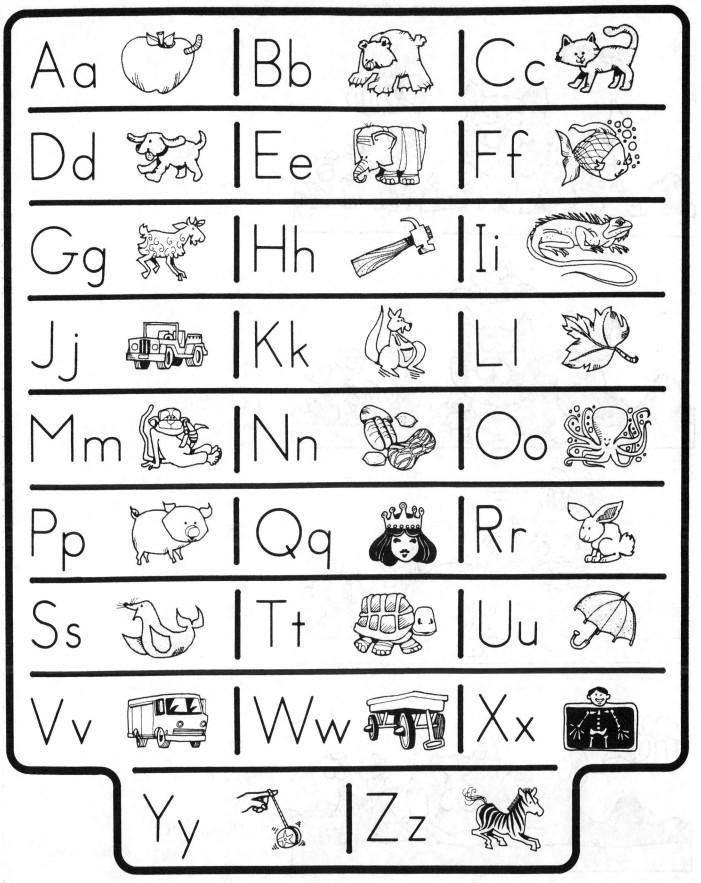

Here Is Bibs

Here is Bibs.
Who is Bibs? Where is she?

Look, Bibs.
What is flying around Bibs's head? How do you think Bibs feels about the bee?

Look, Bibs, look.
What is Bibs doing?

Here is Bibs.
How does Bibs feel now? What will she do next?

Picture Interpretation and Guided Reading (For All Stories): Introduce students to Bibs, a playful kitten who is the main character throughout the book. Encourage them to look at the pictures and to tell what is happening. Have them relate what they see to their own experiences. Anticipate the vocabulary needs of the group. Recognition of words in the story may be developed by writing key words on the chalkboard as the pictures are discussed. Let students read the story silently. Help them with words they do not recognize. Then have students read the story orally. The teacher annotations may be used to guide discussion.

1. b

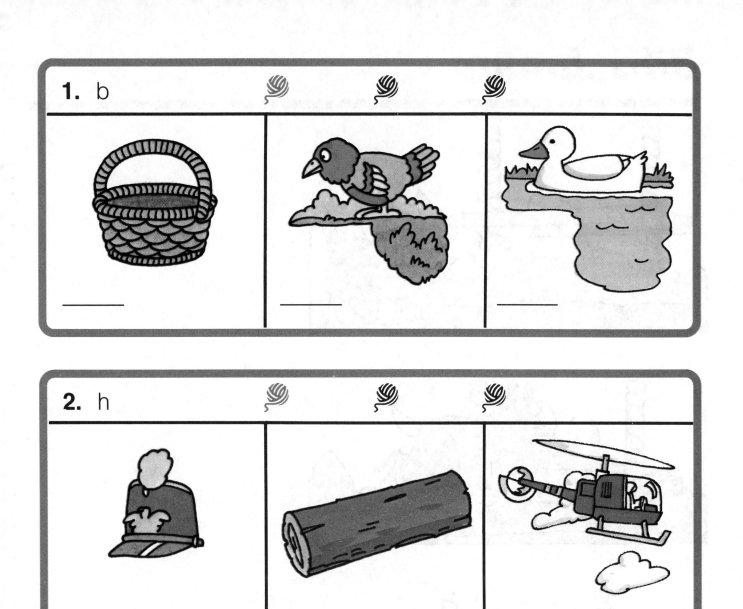

2. h

3.

Initial Consonants (1–2): Review the sounds of **b** and **h**. Have students name the pictures. Have them write **b** (for item 1) or **h** (for item 2) below each picture whose name begins with that sound. Have them put **X** directly on the picture that does not begin with that sound.
Sequence (3): Have students look at all three pictures. Direct them to write **1** below the event that would happen first, **2** below the event that would happen second, and **3** below the event that would happen third.

95

Bibs Jumps

Bibs looks.
What is Bibs looking at? What do you think the ropes are attached to?

Bibs jumps.
Why is Bibs jumping?

See Bibs.
What is happening now? How do you think Bibs feels?

Jump, Bibs, jump.
Why is Bibs jumping off the swing? Do you think Bibs will jump on the swing again? Why or why not?

1. l

_____ _____ _____

2. s

_____ _____ _____

3.

Here is Bibs.
See Bibs jump.

4.

Bibs jumps.
Bibs looks.

Up, Down

See Bibs walk.
What is Bibs stepping on?

Bibs walks up.
What will happen if Bibs walks all the way to the other end of the teeter-totter?

Look down, Bibs.
What is happening now?

Bibs jumps down.
Why is Bibs jumping down? Do you think Bibs will walk up a teeter-totter again?

98

1. d

_____   _____   _____

2. w

_____   _____   _____

3.	Bibs walks up.	yes	no
4.	Bibs jumps up.	yes	no
5.	Bibs looks down.	yes	no
6.	Bibs jumps down.	yes	no

Initial Consonants (1–2): Review the sounds of **d** and **w.** Have students name the pictures. Have them write **d** (for item 1) or **w** (for item 2) below each picture whose name begins with that sound. Have them put **X** directly on the picture that does not begin with that sound.
Facts and Details (3–6): Introduce the words **yes** and **no.** Have students read each sentence and, based on the story events, circle the correct answer.

Jump Up! Jump Up!

Bibs looks up.
She jumps up.

What does Bibs see on the table? Why is Bibs jumping?

See Bibs look.
She looks down.

What is Bibs doing? Why isn't she eating the salad?

Bibs jumps up.

What has happened?

Look at Bibs.

What is Bibs doing now? How long will Bibs stay on the table?

1. k

2. a

3. Look at Bibs walk.
Look at Bibs jump.

4. Bibs jumps up.
Bibs jumps down.

Initial Consonants (1): Review the sound of the letter **k.** Have students name each picture. Direct them to write **k** below each picture whose name begins with the **k** sound. Have them put **X** directly on the picture that does not begin with the **k** sound.

Short Vowels (2): Review the sound of short **a.** Have students name each picture. Direct them to write **a** below each picture whose name has the short-**a** sound. Have them put **X** directly on the picture that does not have the short-**a** sound.

Picture Clues (3–4): Direct students to read the sentences in each box and circle the sentence that best describes the picture.

Bibs Sees Bibs

Bibs looks.
Bibs sees something.

What is Bibs looking into? What does she see?

She looks at it.
It looks at Bibs.

What does Bibs think she sees?

Bibs jumps up.
It jumps up.

How does Bibs feel about what she sees?

See Bibs run.
See it run.

Why is Bibs running? How many kittens do you see running? How many kittens are really running?

102

1. r

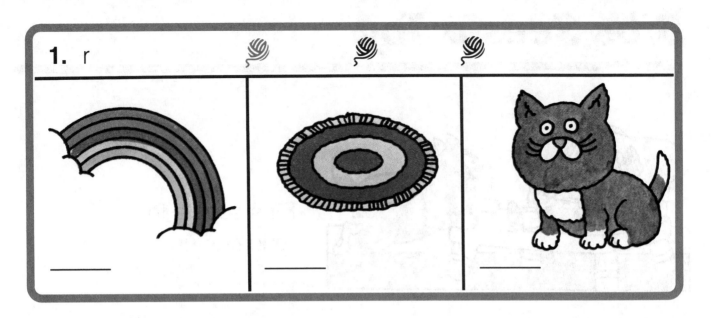

_____   _____   _____

2.

3.

4. walk   jump   run   it

5.

_____   _____   _____

Initial Consonants (1): Review the sound of the letter **r.** Have students name each picture. Direct them to write **r** below each picture whose name begins with the **r** sound. Have them put **X** directly on the picture that does not begin with the **r** sound.

Classification (2–4): Have students look at all four pictures or words in each row and circle the three that belong together. You may wish to guide students through the completed example.

Sequence (5): Have students look at all three pictures. Direct them to write **1** below the event that would happen first, **2** below the event that would happen second, and **3** below the event that would happen third.

Bibs Sees a Toy

Bibs sees a toy.
She jumps up.

What kind of toy has Bibs found? To whom do you think it belongs?

Bibs can play.
Can the toy play?

What does Bibs want the doll to do?

Bibs plays and plays.

What is Bibs doing now? Why?

She jumps down.

How is the doll different from when Bibs found it? How do you think the owner will feel about Bibs and the doll?

1. t

___   ___   ___

2. e

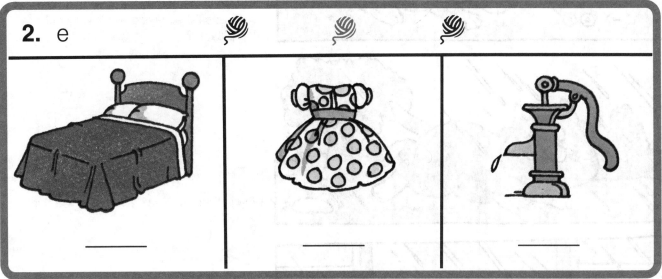

___   ___   ___

3.

It can jump.
It is Bibs.

4.

Bibs is a toy.
She can play.

Initial Consonants (1): Review the sound of the letter **t.** Have students name each picture. Direct them to write **t** below each picture whose name begins with the **t** sound. Have them put **X** directly on the picture that does not begin with the **t** sound.
Short Vowels (2): Review the sound of short **e.** Have students name each picture. Direct them to write **e** below each picture whose name has the short-**e** sound. Have them put **X** directly on the picture that does not have the short-**e** sound.
Picture Clues (3–4): Direct students to read the sentences in each box and circle the sentence that best describes the picture.

Run, Bibs

See Bibs play.
She looks up.

What was Bibs playing with? Why did she stop playing?

Run, Bibs, run!

Why is Bibs running? Where do you think she will go?

What can Bibs do now?

Where is Bibs now? How does she feel about being indoors? What do you think she would like to do?

Look at Bibs.
She can sleep.

Why is Bibs sleeping? What might she do when she wakes up?

1. n

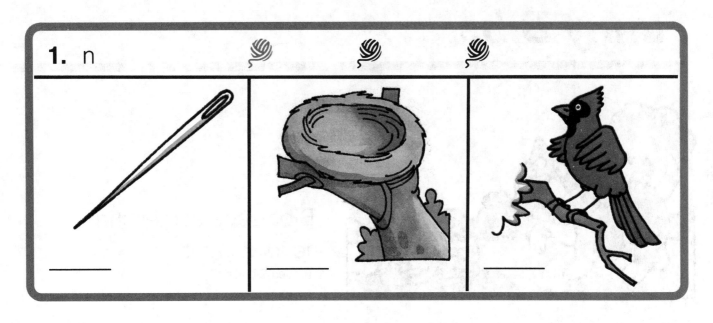

_____   _____   _____

2. j

_____   _____   _____

3. Bibs can _____ up.

play   jump   sleep

4. Bibs _____ a toy.

sees   looks   walks

Initial Consonants (1–2): Review the sounds of **n** and **j.** Have students name the pictures. Have them write **n** (for item 1) or **j** (for item 2) below each picture whose name begins with that sound. Have them put **X** directly on the picture that does not begin with that sound.
Context Clues (3–4): Have students read each sentence and circle the word that best completes the sentence. Then have them write the word in the blank.

Funny Bibs

Bibs sees something.
She looks at it.

What does Bibs see?

See it jump, Bibs.
It jumps here and there.

What do you think Bibs is thinking?

Jump, Bibs, jump!
Bibs looks funny.

What is Bibs doing now?

Bibs will not jump there.
She will not play there.

What can the frog do that Bibs can't do?

1. f

_____   _____   _____

2. a ___ e

3. a ___ e

4. a ___ e

5. a ___ e

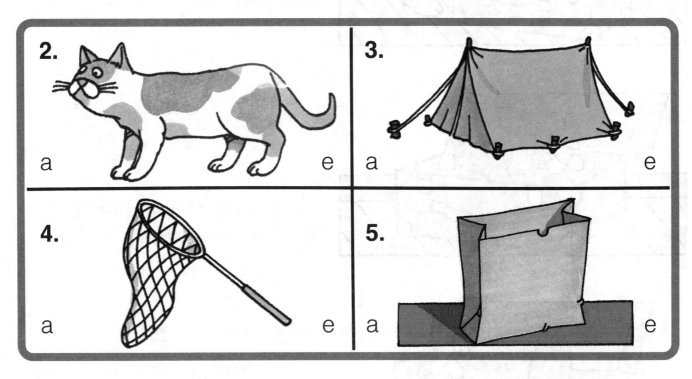

6.

Bibs sees something funny.
It is _____.

7.

Bibs will sleep.
She can sleep in _____.

Initial Consonants (1): Review the sound of the letter **f.** Have students name each picture. Direct them to write **f** below each picture whose name begins with the **f** sound. Have them put **X** directly on the picture that does not begin with the **f** sound.
Short Vowels (2–5): Have students name each picture and listen to the vowel sound. Have them circle the correct vowel below the picture.
Drawing Conclusions (6–7): Have students read the sentences in each box. Then have them circle the picture whose description would best complete the sentence.

Bibs Jumps In

Bibs looks at something.
She jumps in.

What has Bibs found?

Can she play in here?

Why is Bibs jumping into the trunk?

She can't walk in here.
She can't run in here.

What is Bibs trying to do?

Bibs can sleep here.
See Bibs sleep.

Does Bibs like being in the trunk? How
can you tell?

1. z

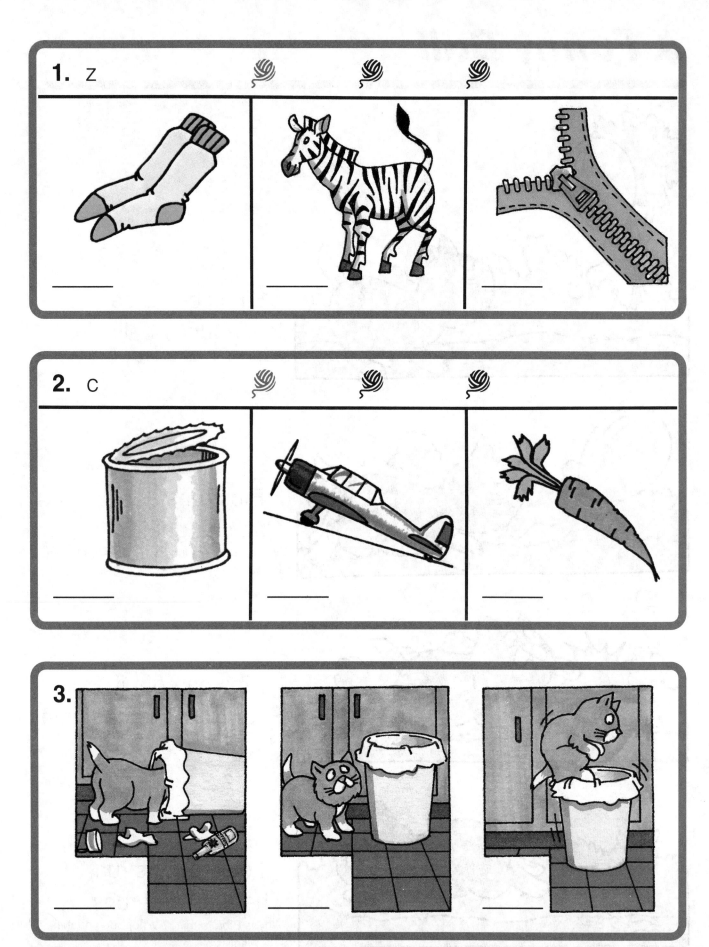

2. c

3.

Initial Consonants (1–2): Review the sounds of **z** and hard **c.** Have students name the pictures. Have them write **z** (for item 1) or **c** (for item 2) below each picture whose name begins with that sound. Have them put **X** directly on the picture that does not begin with that sound.
Sequence (3): Have students look at all three pictures. Direct them to write **1** below the event that would happen first, **2** below the event that would happen second, and **3** below the event that would happen third.

A Funny Ball

Bibs sees a ball.
It is a funny ball.

What kind of "ball" does Bibs see?

Bibs runs.
Can she get it?

Why is Bibs running? Why does Bibs want the balloon?

Bibs can get it.
Pop! Now she can't play.

What made the balloon pop? How does Bibs feel?

Look at Bibs run.
She runs and runs.

Why is Bibs running? Where do you think she will go?

1. p

2. i

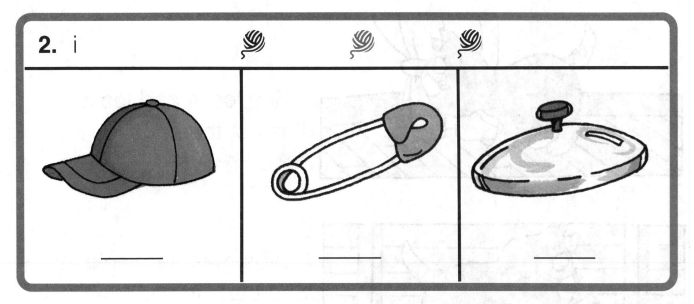

3.

Bibs plays ball.
Bibs sees it pop.

4.

Bibs sees a toy.
Bibs can't get down.

Initial Consonants (1): Review the sound of the letter **p.** Have students name each picture. Direct them to write **p** below each picture whose name begins with the **p** sound. Have them put **X** directly on the picture that does not begin with the **p** sound.
Short Vowels (2): Review the sound of short **i.** Have students name each picture. Direct them to write **i** below each picture whose name has the short-**i** sound. Have them put **X** directly on the picture that does not have the short-**i** sound.
Picture Clues (3–4): Direct students to read the sentences in each box and circle the sentence that best describes the picture.

Bibs Wants Something

Bibs wants something.
Is it here?

Where is Bibs looking? What might she be looking for?

She looks and looks.
It is not there.

Where is Bibs looking now?

Bibs runs and looks.
She can't find it.

Where is Bibs looking now? Is Bibs looking for something big or small? How can you tell?

Here is the doll!
Now Bibs can play.

What did Bibs find? What do you think Bibs will do next?

1. o

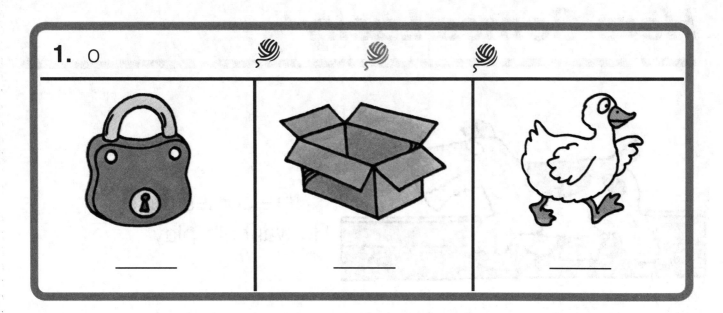

____ ____ ____

2.

3.

4. pop   up   down   in

---

5. Bibs wants up.
What will she do?

walk
sleep
jump

6. Bibs wants to play.
What will she do?

jump at a ball
look at a can
sleep and sleep

Short Vowels (1): Review the sound of short **o.** Have students name each picture. Direct them to write **o** below each picture whose name has the short-**o** sound. Have them put **X** directly on the picture that does not have the short-**o** sound.
Classification (2–4): Have students look at all four pictures or words in each row and circle the three that belong together.
Predicting Outcomes (5–6): Have students read the sentences at the top of each box. Then have them circle the word or phrase below that makes sense.

Here Comes Lucky

Here comes Lucky.
He wants to play.

Who is Lucky?

Lucky looks in there.
He wants Bibs.

Why do you think Lucky is looking for Bibs? Where is he looking?

He looks here.
He can't find Bibs.

Now where is Lucky looking? Where do you think Bibs could be?

Bibs sees Lucky.
She jumps out.
Bibs and Lucky can play.

Where was Bibs? Why do you think she got into the basket? What do you think Bibs and Lucky will do now?

1. m

2. v

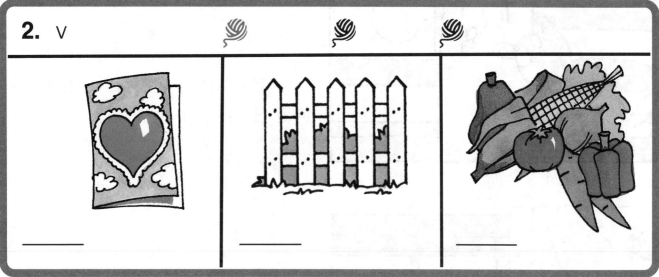

3.

Lucky comes out.
He jumps up and down.

4.

Lucky can't find the ball.
He wants the ball.

Initial Consonants (1–2): Review the sounds of **m** and **v.** Have students name the pictures. Have them write **m** (for item 1) or **v** (for item 2) below each picture whose name begins with that sound. Have them put **X** directly on the picture that does not begin with that sound.
Picture Clues (3–4): Direct students to read the sentences in each box and circle the sentence that best describes the picture.

This Way and That

Something comes in.
It goes to Bibs.

Why does Bibs have one eye closed and one open? What does the dotted line show?

It goes this way and that.
Will Bibs get it?

What is Bibs doing? Why? Do you think she will get the bug?

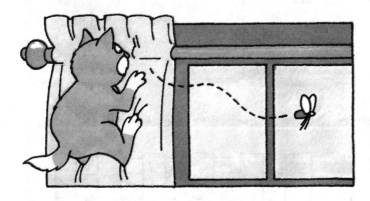

Up and up it goes.
Up and up Bibs goes.

Why can't Bibs get the bug?

Bibs can't get it.
Now Bibs wants down.

How do you think Bibs will get down?

118

1. y

2. g

3. Lucky can't _____ Bibs.

　　　　run　　find　　pop

4. Lucky can _____ the ball.

　　　　walk　　look　　get

Lucky Jumps In

Bibs and Lucky run.
Lucky runs fast.

Who can run faster—Bibs or Lucky? How
do you know?

Lucky jumps.
He jumps into something.

What is Lucky jumping into? Why isn't
Bibs in this picture?

Bibs can't see Lucky.
She looks and looks.

Why isn't Lucky in this picture?

Lucky jumps out.
Bibs looks funny.

Why does Bibs look funny? What do you
think Bibs and Lucky will do now?

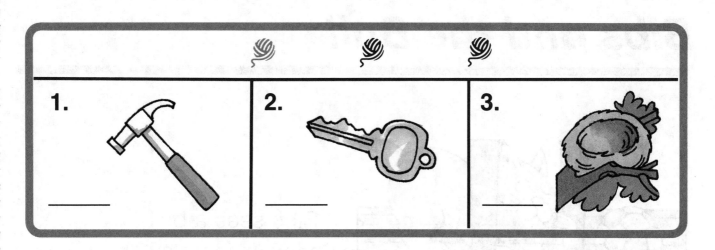

1. ____

2. ____

3. ____

4. i   o

5. i   o

6. i   o

7. i   o

8. ____ runs fast.   Bibs   Lucky

9. ____ jumps into something.   Bibs   Lucky

10. ____ looks and looks.   Bibs   Lucky

11. ____ jumps out.   Bibs   Lucky

Initial Consonants (1–3): Have students name each picture, listen to the beginning sound, and write the beginning letter below the picture.
Short Vowels (4–7): Have students name each picture and listen to the vowel sound. Have them circle the correct vowel below the picture.
Facts and Details (8–11): Have students read each sentence and, based on the story events, circle the correct answer.

Bibs and the Ball

Bibs sees a ball.
She wants to play.
Where is the ball? What is Bibs doing?

Bibs plays with the ball.
She runs and jumps on it.
Why is Bibs jumping on the ball?

Bibs plays and plays.
She rolls over with the ball.
Do you think Bibs is having fun?

Bibs can't get the ball.
Now she can't play.
Why can't Bibs get the ball? Who could
help her get it?

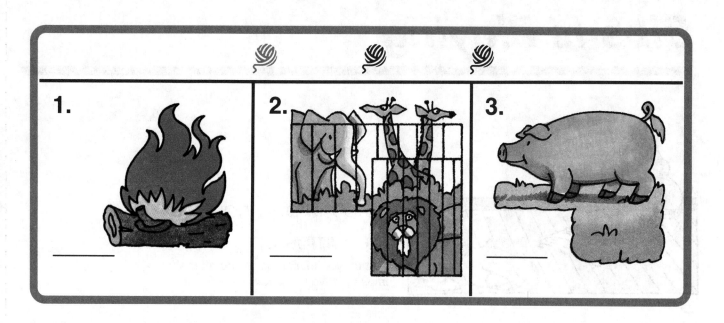

1. _____

2. _____

3. _____

4. u

_____   _____   _____

5. Lucky rolls _____.

      out   down   over

6. Lucky _____ the ball.

    goes   rolls   plays

Initial Consonants (1–3): Have students name each picture, listen to the beginning sound, and write the beginning letter below the picture.
Short Vowels (4): Review the sound of short **u.** Have students name each picture. Direct them to write **u** below each picture whose name has the short-**u** sound. Have them put **X** directly on the picture that does not have the short-**u** sound.
Context Clues (5–6): Have students read each sentence and circle the word that best completes the sentence. Then have them write the word in the blank.

Bibs Is Playing

Bibs is playing.
She jumps up.

What do you think Bibs will do after she jumps up? What is Lucky doing?

Now she jumps down.
Bibs is doing something funny.

Where will Bibs land? What do you think will happen?

See Bibs go.
She goes fast.
Lucky can't see Bibs.

What is happening to Bibs? Why can't Lucky see Bibs?

Look at Bibs!
Look at Lucky!
He sees Bibs now!

Who is surprised? Did Bibs mean to run into Lucky?

124

1. _____

2. _____

3. _____

4. pl

_____   _____   _____

5.

_____   _____   _____

Initial Consonants (1–3): Have students name each picture, listen to the beginning sound, and write the beginning letter below the picture.
Blends (4): Review the sound of the blend **pl**. Have students name each picture. Direct them to write **pl** below each picture whose name begins with the **pl** sound. Have them put **X** directly on the picture that does not begin with the **pl** sound.
Sequence (5): Have students look at all three pictures. Direct them to write **1** below the event that would happen first, **2** below the event that would happen second, and **3** below the event that would happen third.

125

Lucky Wants to Sleep

Bibs wants to play.
Lucky is sleeping.
What do you suppose Bibs is thinking?

Stop that, Bibs!
Do not play there.
Lucky is sleeping.
What is Bibs doing? Why?

Lucky is looking at Bibs.
Stop playing, Bibs!
Lucky wants to sleep.
What is Bibs doing now? Is Lucky still asleep? How do you know?

Bibs stops playing.
She goes to sleep.
Now Lucky can sleep.
Why do you think Bibs has stopped bothering Lucky?

1. sl

_____   _____   _____

2. st

_____   _____   _____

3.

Lucky walks with Bibs.
Lucky runs fast.

4.

Bibs jumps over the doll.
Bibs is sleeping with it.

Blends (1–2): Review the sounds of **sl** and **st.** Have students name the pictures. Direct them to write **sl** (for item 1) or **st** (for item 2) below each picture whose name begins with that sound. Have them put **X** directly on the picture that does not begin with that sound.
Picture Clues (3–4): Direct students to read the sentences in each box and circle the sentence that best describes the picture.

127

Something White

Bibs looks out.
Something white is out there.
It is snow!

Where is Bibs in this picture? What do
you think Bibs is thinking?

Bibs runs out.
She likes the white snow.

How deep is the snow? How can you tell?

Bibs sees a snow house.
She runs and jumps.

Why is Bibs jumping at the snow house?
Who do you think built the snow house?

Now look at Bibs!
She is in the snow.

What has happened here? Did Bibs
expect to land in the snow? What do you
think she will do next?

1. sn

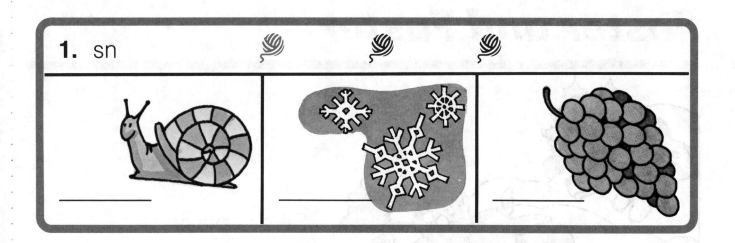

2. a   u

3. e   u

4. i   u

5. o   u

6. The snow is _____.

            fast   white   funny

7. Bibs is sleeping in the _____.

            snow   doll   house

Blends (1): Review the sound of the blend **sn.** Have students name each picture. Direct them to write **sn** below each picture whose name begins with the **sn** sound. Have them put **X** directly on the picture that does not begin with the **sn** sound.
Short Vowels (2–5): Have students name each picture and listen to the vowel sound. Have them circle the correct vowel below the picture.
Context Clues (6–7): Have students read each sentence and circle the word that best completes the sentence. Then have them write the word in the blank.

129

Faster and Faster

Bibs is playing.
Here comes Lucky.
"Get on, Lucky," says Bibs.

What is Bibs sitting on?

Lucky jumps up.
They go down fast.
Faster and faster they go.

What has made the sled start moving?

"Look out!" says Lucky.
"Stop, stop!" says Bibs.

How do Bibs and Lucky feel about the ride? How would you feel?

Look at Bibs and Lucky!
Bibs is on the snow house.
Lucky is in the snow.

What did Bibs and Lucky run into? What do you think they will do now?

1. r

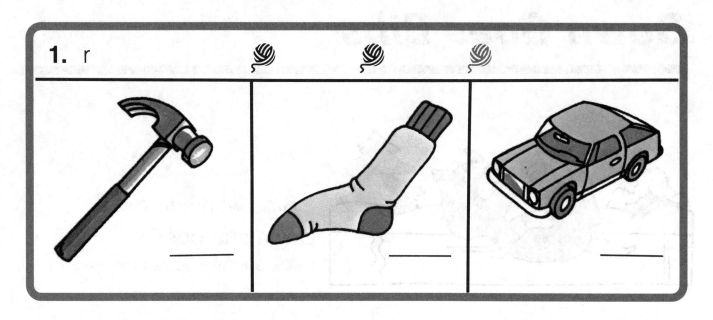

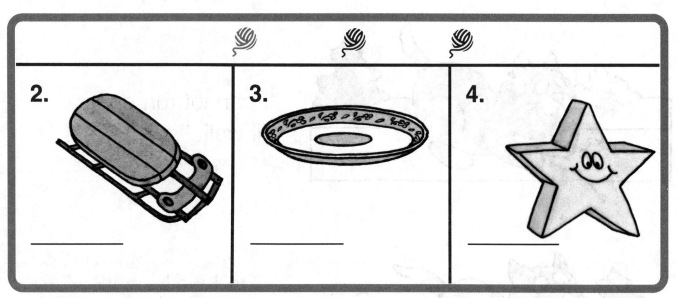

2.

3.

4.

5. Bibs says, "Get on, Lucky."	yes	no
6. Lucky says, "Go faster!"	yes	no
7. Lucky says, "Look out!"	yes	no
8. Bibs says, "Stop, stop!"	yes	no

Final Consonants (1): Review the sound of the letter **r.** Have students name each picture. Direct them to write **r** below each picture whose name ends with the **r** sound. Have them put **X** directly on the picture that does not end with the **r** sound.
Blends (2–4): Have students name each picture, listen to the beginning sound, and write the beginning blend below the picture.
Facts and Details (5–8): Review the words **yes** and **no.** Have students read each sentence and, based on the story events, circle the correct answer.

131

Down Goes Bibs

Bibs wants to run.
Down she goes.

Where is Bibs? Why has she fallen down?

"I cannot run on it.
I will walk," says Bibs.

Why is Bibs just standing in this picture?

"Can I walk on it?
I will not go fast."
Bibs goes down.

What is happening now?

"I cannot run here.
I cannot walk here.
I will go home and play."

Do you think Bibs will fall again before she gets home?

1. t

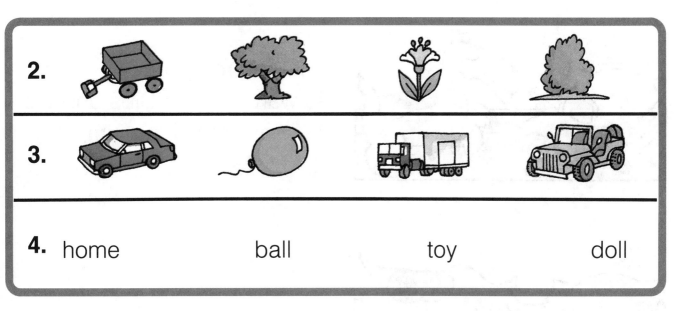

2.

3.

4. home   ball   toy   doll

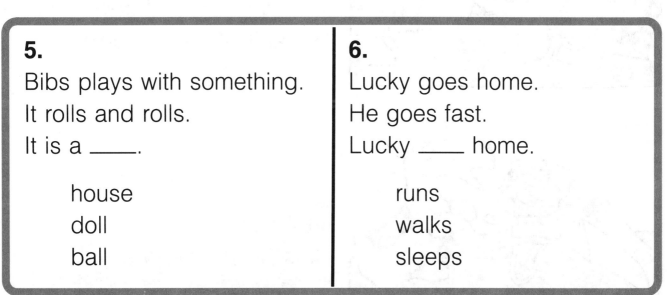

5.

Bibs plays with something.
It rolls and rolls.
It is a ___.

     house
     doll
     ball

6.

Lucky goes home.
He goes fast.
Lucky ___ home.

     runs
     walks
     sleeps

Final Consonants (1): Review the sound of the letter **t.** Have students name each picture. Direct them to write **t** below each picture whose name ends with the **t** sound. Have them put **X** directly on the picture that does not end with the **t** sound.
Classification (2–4): Have students look at all four pictures or words in each row and circle the three that belong together.
Drawing Conclusions (5–6): Have students read the sentences in each box. Then have them circle the word that makes the most sense.

Lucky Finds Bibs

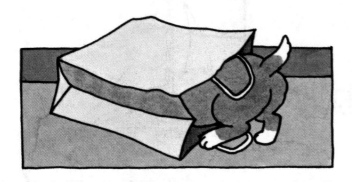

Bibs wants to play.
She sees something she likes.
She goes into it to play.

What is Bibs crawling into?

Here comes Lucky.
He wants to find Bibs and play.
He sees something jumping.

What is the bag doing? What does Lucky think?

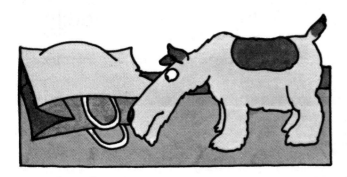

It jumps up and down.
"What is it?" says Lucky.

What is Lucky doing?

Bibs jumps out.
"It is Bibs!" Lucky says.

How does Lucky feel about finding Bibs?

1. tr

_____ _____ _____

2. _____   **3.** _____   **4.** _____

5.

Bibs sees snow.
She likes snow.
What will Bibs do?

    go out to play
    go to sleep
    play in the house

6.

Lucky wants the ball.
It is in his house.
What will Lucky do?

    find Bibs
    go home
    get a doll

Blends (1): Review the sound of the blend **tr.** Have students name each picture. Direct them to write **tr** below each picture whose name begins with the **tr** sound. Have them put **X** directly on the picture that does not begin with the **tr** sound.
Short Vowels (2–4): Have students name each picture, listen to the vowel sound, and write the vowel below the picture.
Predicting Outcomes (5–6): Have students read the sentences at the top of each box. Then have them circle the phrase below that makes sense.

Bibs Plays Ball

Bibs sees a little ball.
"It is a funny ball," she says.

What kind of toy has Bibs found? What is
she going to do with the ball?

Bibs likes the funny ball.
"I will play with it," she says.
The ball goes up and down.

Why does the ball go up and down?

Bibs plays and plays.
She runs with the little ball.
She runs fast.

Does Bibs know what might happen if she
runs with the ball?

"That is not funny," Bibs says.
"I will not play with that."

What lesson did Bibs learn?

1. p

2.

3.

4.

5. The ball is ___.	white	little
6. Bibs ___ the ball.	rolls	likes
7. Bibs runs ___ with the ball.	home	fast
8. "That is not ___," Bibs says.	funny	little

Final Consonants (1): Review the sound of the letter **p.** Have students name each picture. Direct them to write **p** below each picture whose name ends with the **p** sound. Have them put **X** directly on the picture that does not end with the **p** sound.
Short Vowels (2–4): Have students name each picture, listen to the vowel sound, and write the vowel below the picture.
Facts and Details (5–8): Have students read each sentence and, based on the story events, circle the correct answer.

137

A Tree Home

Something is in the tree.
Bibs cannot see it.
She runs up the tree.

Why is there a hole in the tree? Why is
Bibs climbing the tree?

A squirrel looks out.
"Why are you in here?" says Bibs.

Is Bibs surprised to see an animal looking
out of the hole?

"This is my home," it says.
The squirrel goes into the tree.

Do you think the squirrel is afraid of Bibs?
Is Bibs afraid?

Bibs looks in.
"I can't get in," says Bibs.
"This is a funny home!"

Where is the squirrel now? What do you
think Bibs will do next?

1. l

2. fl

3.

Bibs is in a tree.
She wants to go home.
What will Bibs do?

    jump up
    look at a squirrel
    jump down

4.

A squirrel is playing.
It wants to sleep.
What will the squirrel do?

    run up a tree
    play with a doll
    jump in the snow

Final Consonants (1): Review the sound of the letter **l.** Have students name each picture. Direct them to write **l** below each picture whose name ends with the **l** sound. Have them put **X** directly on the picture that does not end with the **l** sound.
Blends (2): Review the sound of the blend **fl.** Have students name each picture. Direct them to write **fl** below each picture whose name begins with the **fl** sound. Have them put **X** directly on the picture that does not begin with the **fl** sound.
Predicting Outcomes (3–4): Have students read the sentences at the top of each box. Then have them circle the phrase below that makes sense.

Down Goes the Duck

Bibs sees a white duck.
The duck goes here and there.

Where is Bibs? Do you think Bibs has
seen a duck before?

Down goes the duck.
Bibs looks and looks.

Why might the duck be going under the
water? How does Bibs look?

"Where are you?" says Bibs.
"Duck, duck, I can't see you!"

How can you tell that the duck is still
there?

"Here I am," says the duck.
"I am a duck, Bibs.
I can go under the water."

Do you think Bibs and the duck will play
together? Discuss.

140

1. n

2. k

3.

Lucky is playing.
He plays under a tree.
Something jumps down.
What is it?

    a duck
    a squirrel

4.

The duck goes this way.
The duck goes that way.
Now Bibs can't see it.
Where is the duck?

    It is under the water.
    The duck is with Bibs.

Final Consonants (1–2): Review the sounds of **n** and **k.** Have students name the pictures. Have them write **n** (for item 1) or **k** (for item 2) below each picture whose name ends with that sound. Have them put **X** directly on the picture that does not end with that sound.
Drawing Conclusions (3–4): Have students read the sentences at the top of each box. Then have them circle the phrase or sentence below that makes the most sense.

The Kite String

Bibs finds something.
It is a kite with string.
Bibs likes the kite string.

What has Bibs found? To whom do you
think the kite belongs?

She wants to play with it.
She goes under the string.
She rolls over the string.

What is Bibs doing?

Bibs rolls over and over.
The string rolls and Bibs rolls.
Now Bibs is in the string.

What happens each time Bibs rolls over?

"I can't play," says Bibs.
"I do not want this string."

How might Bibs get untangled from the
string?

142

1. s

2.

3.

4.

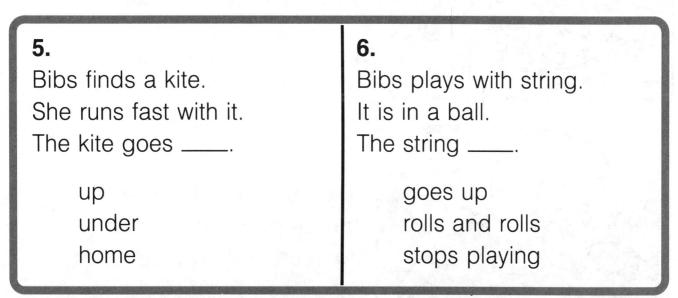

5.

Bibs finds a kite.

She runs fast with it.

The kite goes _____.

    up

    under

    home

6.

Bibs plays with string.

It is in a ball.

The string _____.

    goes up

    rolls and rolls

    stops playing

Final Consonents (1): Review the sound of the letter **s.** Have students name each picture. Direct them to write **s** below each picture whose name ends with the **s** sound. Have them put **X** directly on the picture that does not end with the **s** sound.
Short Vowels (2–4): Have students name each picture, listen to the vowel sound, and write the vowel below the picture.
Predicting Outcomes (5–6): Have students read the sentences at the top of each box. Then have them circle the word or phrase below that makes sense.

The Turtle and the Kite

Bibs sees a turtle.
"Look at my kite," Bibs says.
"Do you want to fly it?"
To whom does Bibs want to give the kite?

"Run fast with it," Bibs says.
"Run faster and faster!"
What is the turtle trying to do?

The turtle can't run fast.
The kite comes down.
The string is on the turtle.
Why did the kite come down? How does
Bibs feel about this?

Bibs runs with the kite.
The kite goes up.
"You can fly it now," Bibs says.
How did the kite get back into the air? Is
Bibs a good playmate? How can you tell?

1. _____

2. _____

3. _____

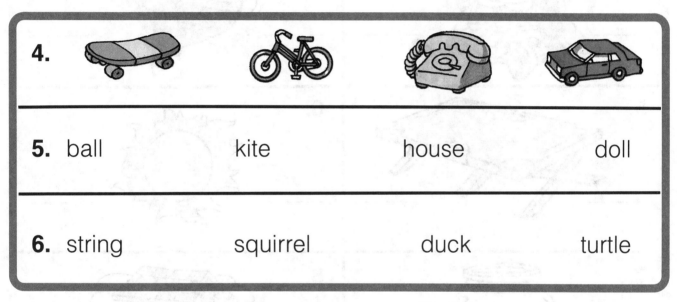

4.

5. ball   kite   house   doll

6. string   squirrel   duck   turtle

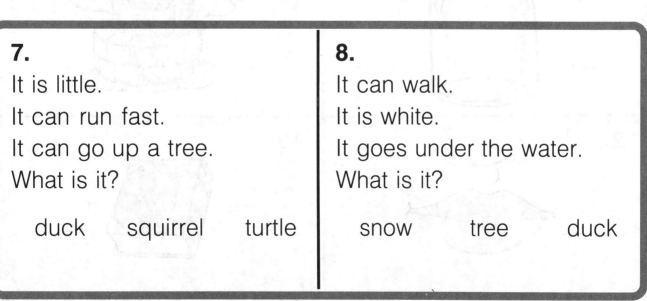

7.

It is little.
It can run fast.
It can go up a tree.
What is it?

duck   squirrel   turtle

8.

It can walk.
It is white.
It goes under the water.
What is it?

snow   tree   duck

Blends (1–3): Have students name each picture, listen to the beginning sound, and write the beginning blend below the picture.
Classification (4–6): Have students look at all four pictures or words in each row and circle the three that belong together.
Drawing Conclusions (7–8): Have students read the sentences in each box. Then have them circle the word that makes the most sense.

Sounds You Know

1. ___ ___

2. ___ ___

3. ___ ___

4. ___ ___

5. ___ ___

6. ___ ___

7. ___ ___

8. ___ ___

9. ___ ___

10. ___ ___

Initial and Final Consonants (1–10): Have students name each picture and listen to the beginning and ending sounds. Direct them to write the beginning and ending consonants for each picture name in the appropriate blanks.

Words You Know

1.
doll
ball
duck

2.
up
turtle
under

3.
he
tree
see

4.
stop
pop
not

5.
looking
sleeping
jumping

6.
fast
house
pop

7.
to
on
in

8.
duck
squirrel
toy

9.
do
doing
doll

10.
likes
kite
white

playing
something
sleeping

12.
now
snow
home

Word Recognition (1–12): Students who have completed all the stories and exercises in *Bibs* should be able to recognize and understand the words on this page. Have students name each picture and circle the word that names or best describes the picture.

147

Words You Know

1. over you out	**2.** can and run	**3.** is it into	**4.** goes get go
5. are at am	**6.** my now not	**7.** walks wants where	**8.** find fly faster
9. jump look walk	**10.** runs finds funny	**11.** way want what	**12.** comes can't cannot
13. here there this	**14.** string sleep snow	**15.** says sees she	**16.** stops jumps plays
17. will white with	**18.** likes little looks	**19.** that the they	**20.** down doing duck

Sight Vocabulary (1–20): Students who have completed all the stories and exercises in *Bibs* should be able to recognize and understand the words on this page. Direct students to circle the word in each box that you read aloud. Suggested words to pronounce are circled in the Teacher Edition. You may prefer to choose different words to fit the needs of your students.

gold Dog god
on Cat Cami
non dll e Nic
ye -Blue k
s off mom
B ross Dad